Contents

Preface

Under the Government's Circular 4/98 (DfEE 1998[1]), all primary and secondary student teachers, in order to obtain qualified teacher status, are now required to demonstrate that they have a working knowledge of a number of areas. These areas have been identified by the Teacher Training Agency (TTA), which was formally established in September 1994. This book concentrates on the non-school-based 'Other Professional Requirements' of 4/98 (p. 16), requirements which can be dealt with in institutions of Higher Education. These are issues such as:

- pay and conditions;
- teachers' legal liabilities and responsibilities relating, for example, to the Race Relations Act 1976 and the Sex Discrimination Act 1975;
- health and safety;
- child protection;
- appropriate physical contact;
- detention;
- bullying;
- liaising with parents and other carers and agencies;
- the role of school governors.

The book aims to provide not only a sound working knowledge of such areas, but also a critical insight into them. It is thus essential reading for student teachers, teachers, teacher educators, headteachers, school governors and parents and other carers of children and young people.

Mike Cole
March 1999

Note

[1] Department for Education and Employment (DfEE) (1998) *Teaching: High Status, High Standards – Requirements for Courses of Initial Teacher Training*. London: DfEE.

Contributors

Dr Mike Cole (University of Brighton) has written extensively on equality and education. His most recent publications include the co-written (with the Hillcole Group), *Rethinking Education and Democracy* (1997), the edited collection, *Human Rights, Education and Equality* (1999) and the co-edited collections, *Promoting Equality in Primary Schools* (1997), *Promoting Equality in Secondary Schools* (1999) and *Postmodernism in Educational Theory: Education and the Politics of Human Resistance* (1999).

Mark Drayton is a primary school governor, with a special interest in Early Years Education. He currently works in the voluntary sector, assisting community organisations, especially tenants associations. He has had wide experience of community groups in Brighton through his work and his Trade Union activity.

Jeff Nixon began his teaching career in a Boys' Secondary Modern School in 1972; he then worked in the Community Studies Department of an 11–8 Comprehensive Community College in West Yorkshire, becoming Head of Department and Head of House. Since 1983 he has worked for the National Union of Teachers at the Union's Regional Office in Haywards Heath, intitially as a District Officer and now as Regional Officer. The contribution he has made to this book is in a personal capacity.

James Parker is a teacher at a large comprehensive school between Brighton and Worthing. After initially leaving school at 16 he returned to education and graduated from Newcastle University with a degree in Politics and History, specializing in American civil rights issues. After living and teaching in Rome, he completed his PGCE at Sussex University and has since taught full time to mixed ability classes of all ages. During this time he has developed a variety of teaching materials, some of which have been used and published by the West Sussex advisory service.

Dee Sweeney has been working within the educational, health and social welfare fields as a freelance consultant since 1993. This work includes research, consultancy, and training. She has also been the District Child Protection Trainer in East Sussex. Prior to this Dee worked within an LEA Advisory Service, specializing in Personal, Social and Health Education. She has taught both in England and abroad as Head of Science and Biology.

Dr David Taubman is interested in the innovative use of 'cultural action' through education to enhance pluralism. He is currently teaching comprehensive school religious education and humanities and heading an international millennium youth project for Oxfam.

Acknowledgements

I would like to thank Kay Jenkins in the Legal and Professional Services Department of the NUT for updating us on current and future legislative issues. Her comments have proved invaluable.

Introduction

'Other Professional Requirements'

Circular 4/98 (DfEE 1998) specifies that all primary and secondary student teachers, in order to obtain qualified teacher status, are now required to demonstrate that they have a working knowledge of a number of areas. Annex A, Section D, of 4/98, 'Other Professional Requirements' (hereafter referred to as A(D)), lists eight requirements, a to h (p. 16 and see Figure 1). Of these, b, c and d are school-based, whereas this book concentrates on the requirements a, e, f, g and h, which can be covered in courses or conferences[1] in institutions of Higher Education. The chapter authors have adopted a broad perspective in considering their themes.

Thus, in Chapters 1 and 2, Jeff Nixon gives some useful advice from a trade union perspective to help student teachers and teachers interpret the various requirements. In addition, in the opening chapter, Nixon covers not only the issues specified in A(D) a(i), he also addresses himself to the importance of 'local agreements'. In Chapter 2, as well as discussing the legal liabilities and responsibilities outlined in A(D) a(ii), the same author also discusses the relevance of the Disability Act of 1995, which is not (but surely should be) part of the A(D) requirements. In Chapter 3, Dee Sweeney outlines the procedures for protecting children and young people from abuse, but also contextualises this crucial aspect of education in terms of teachers' responsibilities as a whole towards those in their care.

David Taubman, in Chapter 4, as well as encouraging teachers to 'take responsibility for their own professional development and to keep up to date with research and developments in pedagogy and in the subjects they teach', points to the distinct lack of a pedagogic tradition in England. Taubman provides both a theoretical account of pedagogy and the practical implications of professional development for the newly qualified teacher.

In Chapter 5, James Parker discusses pastoral and personal safety matters, including bullying, as laid out in A(D)f. However he places these in the context of the Elton Report, one of whose central recommendations was the need to build schools where pupils and students feel safe and secure. In his discussion of bullying, Parker stresses that specific bullying issues such as homophobia, racism

D. OTHER PROFESSIONAL REQUIREMENTS

Primary and secondary

For all courses, those to be awarded Qualified Teacher Status should, when assessed, demonstrate that they:

a. have a working knowledge and understanding of:

  i. teachers' professional duties as set out in the current School Teachers' Pay and Conditions document, issued under the School Teachers' Pay and Conditions Act 1991;

  ii. teachers' legal liabilities and responsibilities relating to:

   - the Race Relations Act 1976;
   - the Sex Discrimination Act 1975;
   - Section 7 and Section 8 of the Health and Safety at Work etc. Act 1974;
   - teachers' common law duty to ensure that pupils are healthy and safe on school premises and when leading activities off the school site, such as educational visits, school outings or field trips;
   - what is reasonable for the purposes of safeguarding or promoting chiidren's welfare (Section 3(5) of the Children Act 1989);
   - the role of the education service in protecting children from abuse (currently set out in DfEE Circular 10/95 and the Home office, Department of Health, DfEE and Welsh Office Guidance *'Working Together: A guide to arrangements for inter-agency co-operation for the protection of children from abuse 1991')*;
   - appropriate physical contact with pupils (currently set out in DfEE Circular 10/95);
   - appropriate physical restraint of pupiis (Section 4 of the Education Act 1997 and DfEE Circular 9/94);
   - detention of pupils on disciplinary grounds (Section 5 of the Education Act 1997).

b. have established, during work in schools, effective working relationships with professional colleagues including, where applicable, associate staff;

c. set a good example to the pupils they teach, through their presentation and their personal and professional conduct;

d. are committed to ensuring that every pupil is given the opportunity to achieve their potential and meet the high expectations set for them;

e. understand the need to take responsibility for their own professional development and to keep up to date with research and developments in pedagogy and in the subjects they teach;

f. understand their professional responsbilities in relation to school policies and practices, including those concerned with pastoral and personal safety matters, including bullying;

g. recognise that learning takes place inside and outside the school context, and understand the need to liaise effectively with parents and other carers and with agencies with responsibility for pupils' education and welfare.

h. are aware of the role and purpose of school governing bodies.

Figure 1 Annex A, Section D, of DfEE Circular 4/98

and sexism should be directly addressed in their own right (see the Conclusion for a discussion of these and other issues).

Dee Sweeney, in Chapter 6, provides a comprehensive overview of the various ways in which schools liaise with parents and other carers and agencies, but also deals with specific issues such as special educational needs, homework, discipline, attendance, behaviour and family learning (an initiative which involves families in the education of their children).

In the final chapter, as well as looking at the role and purpose of school governing bodies, Mark Drayton gives an historical overview and lays out some of the current roles, purposes and responsibilities of school governors. Finally, he questions whether governors are able to deliver effectively on behalf of the school. He asks, 'Just who are school governors anyway?'.

The issues addressed in A(D) are important in their own right, but they also need to be seen in the light of both New Labour's policy on education as a whole, and a different agenda which places equality firmly alongside high standards. These contexts are examined in the remainder of this Introduction, while the Conclusion considers future additions to the 'Other Professional Requirements'.

The New Labour project in education

Our brief, in this book, is to provide information for teachers, student teachers and others. In order to do this, we have outlined Government requirements and recommendations, many of which would be necessary whatever the political complexion of the government. However, we need to look at the ideology underpinning the New Labour project if we are to understand *their* intentions and purposes with respect to Circular 4/98.

From the end of the Second World War up to the mid 1970s (an age of relative social consensus) the labour market was characterised by relative security – 'full employment', employment security (e.g. protection against arbitrary dismissal), job security (an occupation or a trade for life), work security (limits on working time and unsociable hours), skill reproduction security (apprenticeships), income security and security of representation (e.g. through trade unions) (Standing 1997, pp. 8–9).

The Thatcher years broke this social democratic consensus in the interests of global capitalism, moving from a mixed economy to a free market one (with all that that entailed). New Labour is continuing this trend in the wake of the rejection of Thatcherism for its excesses – perhaps necessary at the time precisely to 'break the mould' of British politics. Under the declared pressures of 'globalisation', and the more recent and aligned 'need' for modernisation (Cole 1998), relative stability has been replaced by employment insecurity or flexibility in the operation of flexible labour markets. Thus, in the Foreword to *Excellence for Everyone* (Labour Party 1995), Education Secretary David Blunkett proclaimed that '[t]here will only be well-paid jobs in the future for those who are well-educated, highly skilled, confident and *flexible*' (my emphasis). As Richard Hatcher points out, the Education Secretary failed to admit that there would be many low-skill, low-pay jobs as well, and that good education qualifications would not guarantee a commensurate job, or indeed any job at all (Hatcher 1996, p. 30).

Since globalisation is seen as a central and irreversible fact of life, the 'modernising' project of New Labour means adapting to it (Hatcher 1997, p. 2; see also Leys 1996a, b). Whereas for socialists, including those aligned with 'old Labour', global capitalism represents an obstacle to social progress, for New Labour, the injustices of capitalism need to be resolved by working *with* the market rather than *against* it (Hatcher 1997). The role of the state, therefore, is not to intervene against the market ('old Labour'), but to '"shape advantage" to improve labour market performance, trade balance and competitiveness' (Albo 1997 cited in Hatcher 1997, p. 2). One of the most potentially effective levers available to the Government is the education and training of the workforce – hence the centrality of education (Hatcher 1997, p. 2).

Recent reaffirmations by the Prime Minister serve to reinforce Hatcher's analysis. In an interview with the *Guardian*, Tony Blair sketched out what he called 'five clear principles of the centre-left', two of which were:

> stable management and economic prudence because of the global economy [and] changing the emphasis of government intervention so that it deals with education, training and infrastructure and not things like industrial intervention or tax and spend (Blair 1998, p. 3).[2]

Continuous technological change, a key feature of the modernisation agenda, needs highly trained and flexible employees. The only way to achieve this is via competition, so the organising principle for New Labour, as it was for its predecessors in government, is economic competitiveness. This is believed to be achieved by an 'improvement in standards'.

An egalitarian project in education

The New Labour project of Official School Improvement (OSI) is thought by some to be seriously flawed – 'rhetoric about technical improvement in schools, without reference to the notion of equality' (Hatcher 1998a, b). Hatcher has outlined the essence of OSI and contrasted it with an agenda to promote equality – an egalitarian model (see Figure 2). This model is also concerned with improving standards, but as part of a totally different agenda.

The issues addressed in this book can be seen as purely *practical* requirements for teachers. In this Introduction, it is argued that they need to be viewed in a wider context, in the light of New Labour's overall project in education. They need also to be viewed, however, in the light of a possible future educational project, one which places *equality* firmly alongside *standards* on the agenda of progressive educational change in Britain.

OSI	An egalitarian position
High standards	High standards and a focus on social equality of outcomes
Education for exams	Education for emancipation as well as education for exams
Inflated notion of the ability of schools to compensate for society	Social justice in schools closely linked to social justice in the wider society
Schools seen as neutral	Schools are not neutral and often reproduce inequalities
Low level of spending on schools	Increased funding
A hierarchical and selective schooling system	A comprehensive, non- selective system
Ability grouping	Mixed ability grouping
Social class, gender, ethnicity, sexuality and disability are marginalised or ignored	These issues are central
The curriculum as ideologically neutral	The curriculum reproduces dominant ideologies
Authoritarian managerialism	Grassroots democracy

Figure 2 (adapted from Hatcher 1998a)

Notes

1. The University of Brighton holds conferences for all of its first year student teachers and for its PGCE students, as an introduction to these requirements. Experience has shown this to be a very successful and popular means to address them.
2. The last three of the 'five principles' are 'the reform of the welfare state'; 'reinventing government, decentralisation, opening up government so that what counts is what works' and 'internationalism [rather than] isolationism' (Blair 1998, p. 3).

Bibliography

Blair, T. (1998) 'The next step: a blueprint for New Labour's world role', *The Guardian*, 7 February.

Cole, M. (1998) 'Globalisation, Modernisation and Competitiveness: a critique of the New Labour Project in Education', *International Studies in the Sociology of Education*, **8**(3) p. 315–332

Department for Education and Employment (DfEE) (1998) *Teaching: High Status, High Standards – Requirements for Courses of Initial Teacher Training*. London: DfEE.

Hatcher, R. (1996) 'The limitations of the new social-democratic agendas: class, equality and agency', in Hatcher, R. and Jones, K. (eds) *Education after the Conservatives.* Stoke-on-Trent: Trentham Books.

Hatcher, R. (1997) 'Labour's Educational Policy: Implications For Social Justice'. Paper presented at the British Educational Research Association's Annual Conference, University of York, 11–14 September.

Hatcher, R. (1998a) 'Official School Improvement and Equality', *Socialist Teacher,* **65**, Spring, 16–19.

Hatcher, R. (1998b) 'Labour, Official School Improvement And Equality', *Journal of Education Policy,* **13**(4), 485–99.

Labour Party (1995) *Excellence for Everyone.* London: The Labour Party.

Leys, C. (1996a) 'The British Labour Party's Transition from Socialism to Capitalism', in Panitch, L. (ed.) *Are There Alternatives? Socialist Register.* London: Merlin Press.

Leys, C. (1996b) 'On Top Of The World', *Red Pepper* **25**, 5–21.

Standing, G. (1997) 'Globalization, Labour Flexibility and Insecurity: The Era of Market Regulation', *European Journal of Industrial Relations,* **3**(1) 7–37.

Chapter 1

Conditions of service of schoolteachers

Jeff Nixon

Introduction

What do we mean by conditions of service? In the 1920s and 1930s for example, a woman teacher could be dismissed if she got married or even kept company with men. She was not allowed to ride in a carriage or automobile with any man except her brother or father. She had to be home between the hours of 8 p.m. and 6 a.m., unless in attendance at a school function, and could not leave town without first obtaining the permission of the Board of Trustees. The contract also laid down a non-negotiable dress code which included the prohibition of make-up and stipulated that she should not be seen in places such as ice cream stores (Teacher's Contract 1923: *Women In Education*).

Seventy years later, for those teachers employed in LEA maintained schools, national conditions of service are derived from two basic sources. The first is the *Schoolteachers' Pay and Conditions Document* (DfEE 1998a), often referred to as the 'Blue Book'. This sets out working time, professional duties and conditions of service. The second is *Conditions of Service for Schoolteachers in England and Wales* (CLEA/ST 1985) (the 'Burgundy Book'). This covers national agreements between local education authorities and the teachers' organisations, including such issues as sick pay, sick leave, maternity pay and periods of notice.

Much of what happens in schools is, however, subject to local interpretation. In addition, initiatives may occur either at local or national level which change certain aspects of the teacher's job or may simply emphasise one or a number of items in the conditions of service package at a particular time; for example, the administration in different schools of in-service education and training days (INSET) – the so-called 'Baker Days'. These are named after Kenneth Baker who, as Secretary of State for Education and Science, introduced them in the Teachers' Pay and Conditions Act of 1987. The Act does not specify where or when the INSET days need to be taken, so some schools have operated sessions known as 'twilight training', whereby INSET is carried out during the school's academic year. This is often with the agreement of the staff concerned, with some schools converting days designated as 'Baker Days' into days of school closure. However, if this is the case the school must provide the statutory 190 days of education for all pupils. Teachers are required to be available for work in school for 195 days in any school year (see below).

There may also be local agreements, on issues not covered elsewhere. These may be better or worse than conditions agreed nationally. On the positive side, for example, some LEAs operate a maternity leave and maternity pay agreement that is better than the national one. On the negative side, there exist in the aided or voluntary sector (where the governing body is the employer of teachers) conditions of service which are not in teachers' interests. In Church schools, for example, it is not uncommon to see a clause in the contract of employment that states that the employee should not engage in any activity that may bring the Church into disrepute. This is frequently subject to interpretation at local level within the parish. Here one can see shades of the 1920s contract, with teachers in such schools rarely realising the position they are in until the local parish notable starts asking questions.

In addition, the grant-maintained (GM) sector provides plenty of examples where the conditions of service of teachers have significantly deteriorated; for example, many governing bodies have curtailed the availability of early-retirement packages because the Funding Agency for Schools has squeezed the money available for such schemes. Some GM schools also appear to operate a more rigorous and comprehensive health check on prospective employees than is necessary, and monitor sickness and absence in rather a draconian manner. Despite opposition from teacher unions, there is some evidence to suggest that some LEAs have started to examine such policies, with a view to recommending their introduction in their maintained schools.

All this paints rather a confusing picture. Many teachers enter the profession believing, like many members of the public, that there is in existence a national system of education that is consistent across the country. This is simply not the case. When one adds the differences that exist in sixth-form colleges (independent employers since 1993), City Technology Colleges and the independent sector, and the variations in Scotland and Northern Ireland, the picture becomes even more confused. There are at least four major threats to unified pay and conditions of service arrangements. The first is the pledge by the current Education and Employment Secretary to introduce performance-related pay.

The second is the creation of Education Action Zones (EAZs). EAZs will be able to 'opt out' of national agreements (for a critique of EAZs, see, for example, Cole 1998, Grant 1998, Hatcher 1998).

The third is the creation of 'advanced skills teachers' (DfEE 1998a, p. 56 reproduced as Appendix 2 to this Chapter). Each AST shall be paid on a range of any five consecutive points on the pay spine, which ranges from £26,082 to £41,607 (as at April 1999) with movement up that particular individual range determined by performance which must be a sustained high standard (ibid: 31). The Press labelled this new grade, 'super teacher' and highlighted a potential earning power of £40,000 per annum. It is unclear where the Advanced Skills Teacher (AST) will fit into the normal management structure of schools, and the proposed salary levels will adversely affect the already poor levels of recruitment, particularly in primary schools, to vacancies for headships and deputy headships. The idea that the new grade will recruit high-flying graduates into the teaching profession is particularly debatable; graduates will assess the likelihood of progressing to the higher salary levels against the salaries currently available in other professions and other sectors of the economy.

Schools are dependent on a well-qualified, highly motivated team of staff working together. The AST grade is potentially a divisive and damaging imposition on the education service that will certainly have repercussions in both the short- and long-terms. It would appear that Government has not clearly thought through this controversial strategy in relation to the overall benefits to the education of pupils/students; in particular its stated aim of improving standards.

The National Union of Teachers urged the Government to establish a working party to examine in detail the introduction of the AST grade, but to no avail. Consequently, its General Secretary, Doug McAvoy, wrote to all the other teaching unions and associations, all the LEAs and bodies representing school governors to urge such a working party to oversee the introducion of ASTs. The debate on this issue will thus continue.

Finally, at the end of April 1998 when the Government introduced the idea of Beacon Schools, the then Minister for Schools, Stephen Byers, announced plans for a £1.8 million network of up to 100 such schools. These would be Centres of Excellence committed to sharing the secrets of their success and building partnerships to raise standards.

The extra money for Beacon School status would amount to a maximum of £50,000 per school to cover the extra work arising from the liaison necessary with other schools. The first group of such schools started in the Autumn of 1998 and were selected from the 159 schools named in Her Majesty's Chief Inspector of Schools Annual Report for 1996/97 as 'best performing' schools. Initially, Beacon School status lasts for three years.

As the General Secretary of the NUT, Doug McAvoy, suggested in a press release about the Beacon Schools announcement, the 100 named schools did not represent the sum total of successful schools; those on the list just happened to be there by chance as having recently been inspected and meeting the particular criteria of success on the day. McAvoy went on to say that it was not acceptable to assume these Beacon Schools are better than those which have not had the opportunity to be included in the Oscar-style winners list. He did accept, however, that schools which possess valuable expertise should be expected to share practical support and advice with other schools; such an approach he welcomed and certainly the improved funding to underpin the development should not be criticised.

The extent to which the establishment of a General Teaching Council at the turn of the century will help to address differential pay and conditions within the teaching profession remains to be seen.

The Blue Book: Schoolteachers' Pay and Conditions Document (STPACD) in England and Wales

The genesis of the 'Blue Book' can be found in the national salaries and conditions of service dispute, of 1986–7 (NUT 1987). While the dispute was going on important discussions and negotiations on conditions of service took place under the auspices of the Advisory, Conciliation and Arbitration Service (ACAS). These included class size and hours worked in relation to duties and responsibilities. Up to this time there had been no guidance to quantify the amount of time teachers should spend on the range of professional duties in which they were engaged. Indeed the only reference to the teachers' day, duties and holiday entitlement was contained in the second edition of the Burgundy Book, paragraph 11, which simply stated, 'there are no existing national collective agreements on these matters beyond that affecting the school mid-day break' (CLEA/ST 1985, p. 11)

The Teachers Pay and Conditions Act of 1987, one of the shortest pieces of legislation on the statute book, required the Secretary of State to appoint an Interim Advisory Committee to examine and report on matters referred to it concerning pay and other conditions of employment of teachers in England and Wales. It also empowered the Secretary of State to make orders covering these matters. Before making such orders, the Secretary of State is required to consult with appointed representatives of the LEAs, governors of voluntary schools and schoolteachers. The STPACD has been produced annually and is preceded by a lengthy consultation exercise during which the teacher unions are able to make either joint or separate submissions to a Review Body, set up under the Teachers' Pay and Conditions Act of 1991. Normally, any joint submission is co-ordinated by the National Union of Teachers and time is allocated for the presentation of oral evidence. This provides the General Secretaries of the Unions and Associations the opportunity to address the Review Body directly.

Prior to this system being introduced, *negotiations* on pay and conditions of service took place in the Burnham Committee and the Council of Local Education Authorities (Schoolteacher) Committee, respectively. The Burnham Committee was abolished under the provision of the Teachers' Pay and Conditions Act 1987, whereas CLEA/ST still exists but rarely meets. An Order which provided for conditions of employment to be incorporated into teachers' contracts also came into force in 1987. The National Union of Teachers took no part in the consultations, arguing instead that until the Secretary of State was prepared to discuss the restoration of teachers' negotiating rights, any consultations would simply be a cosmetic exercise.

The conditions of service elements of the Order dealt with teachers' duties and working time only. They contained little safeguard against the excessive workload which was being imposed upon teachers. The Order set down a contractual requirement that teachers should be available for work on 195 days per year of which 190 days would be spent with pupils. It also specified a list of required professional duties (the 1998 list is reproduced in Appendix 1 to this chapter). These cover teaching, related activities, assessments and reports, appraisal, review of further training and development, educational methods, discipline, health and safety, staff meetings, cover for absent teachers, public examinations, management and administration.

This final section 'Administration' contains an important requirement that is worth examining in more detail. The phrase in question implies a responsibility for 'supervising pupils... before, during or after school sessions'. The question of responsibility for pupils before, during and after school session times is an important point and needs clarification. Schools, and head teachers in particular, should make it clear to parents/carers that the supervision of pupils by the school begins and ends at particular times. Many parents/carers may be in the habit of dropping children off at school some time before school begins. The NUT recommends to heads and members that teachers are available to receive pupils ten minutes before the start of the school day and to dismiss them up to ten minutes after the school day ends. Between morning and afternoon sessions, the Union recommends that members are available for five minutes beyond the morning session to supervise pupils going to lunch either on or off the school premises and are available to receive pupils once more five minutes before the start of the afternoon session. It is important that this time forms part of the directed-time element of teachers' professional duties in case an accident occurs. If head teachers include this in the allocation of 1,265 hours of directed time for the year, it would amount to 95 hours of directed time for all teachers in the school year. It may be possible, however, in larger schools to organise this responsibility on a rota basis. Heads should also let parents/carers know in writing that these are the arrangements and that the school can only accept responsibility for the supervision of pupils at particular stated times.

Apart from the obvious concerns about pupil welfare and safety, there are legal implications. Barnes v Hampshire County Council (Local Government Review 1969) concerned a five year old girl who, in 1962, left school before the end of the school day which was known as 3.30 p.m.. The girl should have been met at the school gate by her mother. However on this particular day, the mother had not yet arrived. The children had been told that if no one was there to collect them, then they should return to their teacher. In this case, the girl did not do so and attempted to cross the busy A30 trunk road at a point 250 yards from the school gate. Unfortunately she was involved in an accident which resulted in serious injuries, including partial paralysis of her left arm and foot. A witness heard the accident and telephoned for an ambulance. His emergency call was recorded at the telephone exchange at 3.30 p.m.

Initially the parents' claim for negligence on behalf of their daughter was rejected. However, following a further rejection in the Court of Appeal, the Master of the Rolls, Lord Denning, dissented in the majority judgment and maintained that the school's system depended on the parents being there to meet the children at half past three, and on the school not letting them out until that time. To let them out before the mothers were due to arrive was to release them into a situation of potential danger, and in his view this constituted a breach of duty. Previously, the judges had said that ordinary people in ordinary life do not carry a chronometer;

they did not believe that three to five minutes in the case before them constituted a breach of duty.

The case was referred to the House of Lords who reversed the judgment of the Court of Appeal and awarded damages of £10,000 against the LEA. The Lords agreed with the Master of the Rolls, emphasising that it was the duty of the school authorities not to release the children before the end of the school day. While early release would seldom lead to an accident, forseeably it could do and in this case it did.

It is important to note that, as the employer, it was the LEA which was taken to task in the above example. LEAs have a vicarious liability for the acts or omissions of employees, who are acting in the course of their employment. In these circumstances, LEAs are responsible for the payment of any award of damages or compensation. Under health and safety legislation, it is, however, possible for teachers to be fined, as was a science teacher in 1986. This teacher was fined £500 after the Health and Safety Executive brought a successful case, following investigation of an explosion during a school experiment which resulted in 15 children being taken to hospital. It was believed to be the first prosecution of a teacher under the Health and Safety at Work Act 1974.

Magistrates were told that no safety precautions were taken in the experiment for a class of 12 and 13 year olds, who were showered with sulphuric acid. Fortunately no one was seriously hurt. The teacher admitted failing to take reasonable care to protect children who were in the lesson. The magistrate told the teacher that the consequences could have been disastrous for some, if not all the children in the class. Parents were entitled to feel their children were safe whilst at school. The court heard that the pupils were sprayed with acid after a flask exploded in an experiment to demonstrate the reduction of metal oxide. Although plastic screens and protective spectacles were available at the school, the teacher did not use them. The Health and Safety Inspector reported that many of the children received burns from droplets of acid on their arms and bodies. One of the children was cut by flying glass and the face of one child was only a foot away from the bottle containing the acid. Fourteen of the children taken to hospital were discharged after treatment; one stayed in hospital overnight.

The Health and Safety Inspector said there was no wish to restrict the teaching of science by banning all experiments where there was an element of risk. The inspector believed that potentially dangerous experiments could be done safely, if reasonable precautions were taken. The teacher concerned received a reprimand.

Conditions of service were changed considerably by the Education Reform Act of 1988. This provided for local management of schools (LMS), giving governing bodies much more control and seriously eroding the power of the head teacher and the LEAs. The Act also made provisions for schools to opt out of LEA control and become grant-maintained. The overall effect was to loosen the influence LEAs had on schools and consequently potentially worsen the conditions of service of teachers at local level.

The Burgundy Book: Conditions of Service for Schoolteachers in England and Wales

The Burgundy Book deals with sick pay and sick leave, maternity pay and maternity leave and notice. It also refers to legislation affecting teachers' conditions of service with respect to redundancy payments, unfair dismissal, sex discrimination, trade union membership and activities, time off work, race relations, health and safety at work, premature retirement and medical fitness to teach (including those medical conditions when teachers would be suspended from teaching duties on the grounds of ill-health).

Three other sections of the Burgundy Book are also worthy of note. These are the model procedure to resolve collective disputes, facilities for trade union representatives and the 1968 School Meals Agreement. This agreement was a major breakthrough for teachers in that it allowed teachers the freedom to take a lunch break away from the children and the school. Teachers could no longer be required to undertake supervision at lunch time and that aspect of the conditions of service package remains intact to the present day. There is not much employment law beneficial to the workforce that has survived over thirty years. The 1968 School Meals Agreement was thus an historic landmark for teachers and, in my view, remains so.

Sick pay and sick leave

Teachers' sick pay and sick leave are detailed on a sliding scale entitlement according to length of service. During the first year of service, full pay for 25 working days is granted and, after completion of four calendar months, half pay for 50 working days. This becomes full pay for 50 working days, followed by half pay for 50 working days during the second year and full pay for 75 working days and half pay for 75 working days, during the third year. In the fourth and successive years of service, full pay for 100 working days and half pay for 100 working days is allowed. The scale is described as a minimum; some LEAs have agreed local improvements. LEAs and governing bodies will have the discretion to extend the scheme in particular circumstances although it has to be acknowledged that the introduction of LMS has made that more problematic. It must also be noted that the scale is expressed in terms of working days which means that holiday periods are discounted. However, teachers' pay continues in a holiday period at the rate it was prior to the holiday commencing; this means in fact that the actual time teachers can be on sick leave on full pay is approximately six months when in the fourth or subsequent year of service, followed by six months on half pay.

Teachers are also entitled to Statutory Sick Pay (SSP), a basic entitlement for all employees whatever their job. This is paid for the first 28 weeks of absence, after which State Incapacity Benefit must be claimed from the Department of Social Security. When a teacher is receiving full sick pay, SSP is included in this. When a teacher goes on to half pay, SSP will be paid on top. Teachers in their first year of service who have only a limited entitlement under the scheme will continue to receive SSP after their entitlement to full and half pay has run out.

Maternity leave and maternity pay

Right to maternity leave and pay are dependent upon length of service although all women teachers are entitled to a minimum of 18 weeks maternity leave, regardless of length of service. Women teachers with at least two years' service with one or more LEA are entitled to an extended period of leave of up to 40 weeks. Normally leave before the birth of up to 11 weeks can be taken with 29 weeks of post-natal leave available. Women teachers can work closer to the expected date of the birth should they choose to do so, but they cannot add to the 29 weeks of post-natal leave any of the 11 weeks of pre-natal leave available to them but not taken as leave. Maternity pay is provided on the following basis for the duration of the maternity leave: for the first four weeks of absence, full pay; for the next two weeks 90 per cent of a week's salary, and for the remainder of the 18 week period of absence, half pay. For any remaining period of absence up to the date of return, the woman teacher receives no pay. Women teachers become eligible to receive Statutory Maternity Pay (SMP) in the period after the first six weeks of maternity pay; however it is only paid for 18 weeks and the first six weeks are taken into account in the entitlement calculation. The current rate (January 1999) is £57.50 per week.

A woman teacher has the right to return to her job following the ending of her maternity leave although the employer may, by giving notice in writing, postpone her return by no more than four weeks after the notified date of return. The notice must specify the reason for postponement. The woman teacher must return to her job for at least 13 weeks, which effectively means at least a full term; if she does not comply with this provision she must refund some or all of her maternity pay. This requirement to return for 13 weeks may be reduced at the discretion of the employer. Frequently women teachers choose to reduce the number of hours they work upon return to work following maternity leave. Whilst there is no right to do this under the terms of the Burgundy Book, there are examples which can be quoted from Industrial Tribunal (now Employment Tribunal) decisions that are particularly helpful when women teachers wish to reduce their hours or change from full-time to part-time employment, or to work on a job-share basis. A refusal by employers to accept a request for a reduction of hours or to operate a job-share could give rise to a claim of sex discrimination. This happened with respect to a refusal of job-share by the Governing body of Ellis Guildford Comprehensive School and Nottinghamshire County Council. In March 1996, the Nottingham tribunal agreed that the teacher concerned had been indirectly discriminated against on grounds of her sex because she was refused a request for a job-share following maternity leave. The governors of the school attempted to argue that a job-share would create inconvenience for the school. The tribunal however did not accept this as a justifiable reason for refusing to arrange a job-share. It found that a requirement imposed on a woman teacher to work full-time was 'unanswerable' and amounted to indirect sex discrimination. This and the related case of Mrs Clay v English Martyrs School are considered to be significant decisions that give weight to requests for reduced hours or job-share, when returning to work after maternity leave.

The Burgundy Book is silent on the right to paternity leave. Some LEAs, however, do include it as part of local conditions and agreements, and the NUT has campaigned for its inclusion as part of a package of measures designed to improve the conditions of service of all teachers. As an example of good practice, the NUT as an employer of staff grants ten working days for paternity leave.

Grievance, disciplinary and capability procedures.

The Burgundy Book places an obligation on employers (LEAs and governing bodies in relation to GM schools, voluntary aided schools, sixth-form colleges and City Technology Colleges and schools in the independent sector) to provide teachers with copies of procedures governing the resolution of grievances and discipline. Since Local Management of Schools, governing bodies have usually adopted procedures recommended by the personnel sections of LEAs. It can be argued that all such procedures form part of a teacher's contract of employment and if they are not followed, this could readily give rise to a claim for breach of contract.

As far as teacher capability is concerned, an Occasional Paper written by Dr Caroline Wragg's team at the University of Exeter Teacher Competence Project (Wragg *et al.* 1998) reported interviews conducted with teacher association/union officers which examined the manner in which capability procedures are used by schools and LEAs. The Union officers interviewed agreed that it was their job to ensure that teachers were treated fairly and properly when such procedures were used and that this should include realistic time-scales in order for the teacher to be given adequate support, guidance and encouragement to improve on performance. The four-week fast track approach encouraged by the Minister for Schools, and taken up in the media, gave the public and, to some extent the profession, two false impressions: first that there are too many incompetent teachers, and second, that the Government is doing something about it.

The amendments encouraged by the Government and the DfEE covered one paragraph containing two sentences. Most LEA recommended procedures on capability provide as many as six pages of guidance to head teachers and governors on how to apply such procedures.

Periods of notice

Normally, unless the contract of employment states differently, there are only three dates in the year when teachers can leave a job or be dismissed (except in the case of summary dismissal which can occur at any time and is usually linked to offences that can be described as gross misconduct). The dates are 31 December in the Autumn term, 30 April in the Spring term and 31 August in the Summer term.

Notice must be given by the teacher or the employer on 31 October in the Autumn term, 28 or 29 February in the Spring term and 31 May in the Summer term. If a teacher leaves at the end of the Spring term and has another job to go to that starts at the end of the Easter holiday period, then salary is only paid until the day before the new job commences. However, if the teacher is not going on to work for another employer, salary is paid until 30 April. This is regardless of when Easter falls in that particular year.

If a teacher misses the notice date, the LEA or school may insist that the teacher stays until the end of the following term. In these circumstances, a teacher may apply to the headteacher and/or the Governing body of the school for what is termed 'early release' from contractual obligations. Notice periods for GM schools and sixth-form colleges are usually the same. In the independent sector, a full term's notice may be required in some contracts of employment and in CTCs there are variations to the Burgundy Book notice periods which frequently mean teachers are under a shorter notice period.

All employees acquire rights to more notice as the period of continuous employment increases over the years. The maximum is 12 weeks notice once the period of employment is 12 years or more and the minimum is one week. Thereafter, employees accrue an extra week's notice for every completed year of continuous service. This means that should the employer wish to give notice to terminate the contract and the teacher has, say ten years service, then the period of notice has to be ten weeks, under the provisions of the Employment Rights Act 1996. This provision only operates if it is the employer giving notice; it does not affect the period of notice the teacher has to give in order to leave the job. The statutory notice period can run concurrently with the notice given according to Burgundy Book requirements (see previous paragraph).

Some contracts, particularly those issued to cover maternity leave or long-term absence due to illness, contain a much shorter notice period, usually one week. This is to enable the employer to comply with the rights of the employee who wishes to return to work. For women teachers who are returning to work from maternity leave this is to enable the school and the employer to comply with the Burgundy Book provisions on maternity leave discussed earlier. Similarly, unless there is some doubt about a teacher's fitness to return to work following illness (and in cases where there is doubt, the employers' medical officer or occupational health advisers will be consulted), a teacher who is declared fit to return to work following illness clearly has the right to do so. This obviously has an effect on the contract given to any teacher who covers a long-term sickness absence. That is why the notice period may be as short as one week in such contracts

Local agreements

The third component of the conditions of service package for teachers is contained within whatever local agreements have been negotiated within the LEA or the school (e.g. GM or sixth form college; it is unlikely that negotiated local agreements will exist in the independent sector as recognition of the teaching unions and associations is likely to be problematic). Local agreements normally cover matters not covered in the Burgundy Book, such as time off other than for sickness and maternity leave. Entitlements or guidance to head teachers and governing bodies in exercising discretion on leave of absence covering paternity leave, bereavement, relative's illness, weddings, study leave, moving house and other circumstances are all dependent on local agreements. There will not always be a right to time off for these matters and it may not always be paid leave. The decision on leave of absence may be delegated to the head teacher. This has particularly been the case since the introduction of Local Management of Schools. However, the ultimate decision on the right to leave of absence will rest with the employer, which in most cases will be the LEA.

If, in an LEA school, the head teacher refuses time off for duties and/or activity related to a teacher's role as a trade union representative, the LEA may decide to intervene and advise the head to sanction the request. There is a Code of Practice produced by ACAS (1998), that emphasises leave for such matters should not be unreasonably refused.

Other aspects of teachers' conditions of service that are determined locally are the precise timings of the school day. There are considerable variations between the Key Stages. The amount of contact time in an infant school, for example, may be around five hours, whereas in a secondary school it may be up to 5 hours 45 minutes. It is left to the school to decide the precise timings of the day, the timing of breaks, the length of morning and afternoon sessions and the length of the lunch time. Thus, some schools may operate a very short lunch break of 30 minutes whereas others, mostly primary schools, will allocate one and a half hours. The reason for such a lengthy lunch break will probably be historical and date back to the time when so many children took a school lunch that the school found it necessary to offer more than one sitting because of the size of the school hall and the limited kitchen facilities.

Circular 7/90 (DfEE 1990) provides a framework to manage any proposed changes and gives illustrations of average timings in different types of school. Changes to the school day can only be introduced in September of the school year and parents, the LEAs and other groups with an interest (for example bus companies and taxi firms) need to be consulted and to be given at least three months' notice. It is interesting to note that there is no requirement in the circular to consult teachers. However, it would not be considered good practice to keep teachers out of such discussions and in cases where governing bodies appear to be overlooking the interests and opinions of teachers, other methods and procedures, such as the Grievance Procedure or the Collective Disputes Procedure can be used by the teachers to ensure their views are taken into account and acknowledged.

Contracts of employment

Once a job has been offered and that offer has been accepted, then a legal contract comes into existence, even if there is nothing in writing to confirm the agreement. Head teachers, governing bodies and LEAs are understandably unsympathetic to teachers agreeing to accept a post and then changing their minds (often signalling by implication that something better has been found). The redress of the school, governing body and/or LEA might take a number of different forms. They may threaten to sue the teacher concerned for breach of contract. This is technically possible although unlikely in reality. What is more likely is that expenses for attendance at the interview will not be paid. Some LEAs may take a further step of circulating the name(s) of candidates who cause this sort of inconvenience to schools in the LEA although that practice has lessened since LMS was implemented and governing bodies have much more control over the appointments procedure. Certainly it is not unusual, in the case of student teachers letting down a school or an LEA, for the training institution to be contacted and told about the student who has accepted the offer of a post and then declined it at a later stage.

There are three different types of contract: permanent,[1] temporary, and fixed-term. A temporary contract does not have within it a termination date; sometimes schools and LEAs will issue temporary contracts to teachers, using the phrase 'in the first instance' to suggest that at some point the contract will be made permanent. A teacher on a temporary contract would acquire employment protection rights arguably after one year's service and certainly after two years. Indeed, during 1999, new legislation will grant protection against unfair dismissal to employees with one year's continuous service. Therefore, unless the temporary contract is for a genuinely temporary reason (see below), the employer should be persuaded to transfer the teacher to a permanent contract. Having said that, there have been cases where teachers have experienced year on year temporary contracts for as many as twelve years. Such a long period on temporary contracts almost redefines the word temporary, and is something which trade unions are constantly challenging.

A fixed-term contract is for a defined period and contains a date on which the job will end – normally the three end of term dates referred to in the section on notice periods: 31 December, 30 April and 31 August. Teachers who are offered fixed-term contracts should ask why it is only for a defined period (the same questions should be asked when temporary contracts are offered). Sometimes the justification given is 'for budgetary reasons', and many schools will offer such contracts on a year by year basis. However, what such contracts amount to is pre-selection for redundancy and they have the effect of creating two separate groups within a school: those who are directly at risk of being declared redundant (those on temporary contracts) and the rest of the staff (on permanent or ongoing contracts) who are clearly protected from any initial selection process for redundancy.

The trade unions take the view that fixed-term or temporary contracts should only be used where there is a genuine fixed-term or temporary need which is seen from the outset to be the case. Examples would be contracts that are issued to cover a maternity leave, long-term sickness, secondment of a teacher or where a school needs to cover a vacancy whilst awaiting the release of a teacher from another contract. These examples will be considered legitimate uses of fixed term or temporary contracts. It has been noticeable in recent years, certainly following the introduction of LMS and after Kenneth Clarke as Secretary of State for Education abolished the arrangements for the probationary year, that schools have been using fixed-term and temporary contracts as a device to assess a teacher's suitability for the post. This is an abuse of such contracts and it should not be used to replace a properly-resourced induction period for teachers, particularly for newly qualified teachers (NQTs). Induction was introduced by the DfEE in the Teaching and Higher Education Act 1998, and it is proposed to implement the relevant provisions with effect from September 1999. This should be very helpful in reducing this abuse.

Another worrying aspect that emerged from research on temporary and fixed-term contracts (NUT 1995) is the number of part-time staff on such contracts. Some employers wrongly equate part-time work with temporary contracts. The majority of part-time teachers are women, and issuing only temporary part-time contracts to them as a matter of policy, would be regarded as indirect sex discrimination and could give rise to an Employment Tribunal claim, without any requirement for a continuous service qualifying period. Part-time teachers should also watch out for a variable hours clause in their contracts. This clause is sometimes inserted in an attempt to manage the needs of a school from year to year. In much the same way as full-time contracts may be issued on a fixed-term or temporary basis for 'budgeting reasons', part-time contracts with a variable hours clause may well be used in a similar manner although the variable hours clause disguises that fact. Obviously there are financial implications for teachers who may have their hours of work varied from one year to another or even one term to another; if the hours are reduced the salary reduces as well. Unless the contract specifically deals with the extent of the variation, a part-time teacher could be offered work amounting to 99 per cent in one year (this is effectively full-time apart from 15 minutes in the week) and this could reduce to as little as 10 per cent the following year (one morning or afternoon per week). The effect on salary would be dramatic. In order to offset such drastic variations some LEAs have built ranges of hours into the contracts in order to attempt to guarantee a minimum number of hours per week and consequently make the part-time teacher more financially secure.

Contracts may also contain waiver clauses. One anticipated adverse effect of the Court of Appeal decision on the Seymour-Smith and Perez case is the likelihood that employers will seek to use measures to avoid employment protection obligations. A waiver clause in a contract excludes or undermines rights in law by requiring an undertaking from the employee not to take action for unfair dismissal or redundancy. The Employment Relations Bill introduces a new prohibition on the use of waiver clauses in respect of protection against unfair dismissal. Waiver clauses related to redundancy will, however, remain lawful. The use of such clauses again divides the workforce, separating those with employment protection rights from those who will never acquire such rights. Since employees have very few rights in the first place, to be asked or required to sign away these limited rights is totally unacceptable. The introduction of a General Teaching Council (GTC) will at least oversee abuses of contract law on behalf of the teaching profession, and may even adopt a naming and shaming policy where LEAs and schools attempting to use waiver clauses are identified.

There is one final point to make on contracts. The non-renewal of a fixed-term or temporary contract is, in the eyes of the law, a dismissal. In order to comply with the law, in carrying out the dismissal, the employer should ensure it is done fairly by applying a proper procedure to the process of dismissal. This may mean offering the opportunity to a teacher threatened with dismissal by reason of the non-renewal of a contract to make representations to the governing body or the LEA before notice of non-renewal is given. In addition, an opportunity to appeal against a recommendation to dismiss must be provided. In the maintained sector the appeal hearing must be held prior to the date on which the teacher is given notice; however in the sixth-form sector the appeal can be heard in the notice period but obviously before the date of dismissal. If a teacher is facing the loss of a job and simply forgoes rights to a hearing, perhaps because of ignorance, then employers will be able to abrogate their responsibilities under employment law.

Teachers need to be cautious about contracts and use the experience and expertise of full-time union officers in examining contracts thoroughly. Contracts should not be taken on trust; there are far too many examples of abuses of contract law. It is far too easy to mislead employees in this area of the law.

Salaries

Newly qualified teachers' salaries are dependent on qualification and, in some cases, experience. Good honours graduates, those with a first or second class honours degree or equivalent, receive two mandatory points on the spine. The rest start on the bottom of the pay spine at point 0.

For experience inside or outside teaching, up to a maximum of nine points may be allocated. For good honours graduates, therefore, who begin at point 2, the number of experience points available is seven. Each September, a serving teacher who has worked at least 26 weeks in the previous 12 months will receive an additional spine point, subject to the maximum of spine point 9 being reached. These annual additional spine points are mandatory, provided that the teacher's performance is satisfactory. The onus is upon the school or the LEA to prove that a teacher's performance has been unsatisfactory. This means following a proper procedure and not simply deeming that an additional point is being withheld.

Experience gained outside teaching may include work experience or unremunerated activity such as bringing up a family. The allocation of such spine points is not mandatory; however, governing bodies should always take such experience into account when determining the starting salary of mature entrants.

Up to two points, or three points in Inner London, may be allocated for recruitment and retention purposes. These points are available for use where posts have been difficult to fill; in certain geographical locations for example, or in subjects where there are shortages of teachers. These points must be reviewed every two years. Additional duties and responsibilities (which should be clearly defined in the job description) qualify for up to five additional points. These would be added to the points score for qualification, experience and, where appropriate, recruitment and retention points. In primary schools it is unlikely that posts will attract more than three points because of lack of funds, and also because of the structure of most primary schools. In some secondary schools five point responsibility allowances have replaced the non-mandatory deputy-head positions.

Teachers in special schools and teachers of special needs in mainstream schools may receive up to an additional two points on the pay spine. All teachers in special schools must receive at least one additional spine point.

In addition, up to three points may be allocated for excellence across all areas of performance, but with particular regard to classroom teaching. These spine points must be reviewed every year. Most governing bodies have ignored the 'points for excellence' or simply stated that, in the absence of clear objective criteria to measure 'excellence', the points will not be available. It is widely regarded that the implementation of 'points for excellence' would not be seen as fair by the profession and, in many instances, would be regarded as divisive, particularly if the points were allocated on a 'grace and favour' basis by head teachers.

Teachers in the London area receive one of three London area allowances in addition to the points score which determines the basic pay spine salary. The Inner London Area qualifies for an additional £2,166 per annum; the outer London area, £1,425 and the Fringe Area an extra £555 (December 1998, London Allowance Rates).

It is recommended that before formally accepting a teaching post the spine point at which the teacher will be placed is established. All teachers are entitled to receive, on an annual basis, a statement of the points score applicable to the post held. It is important therefore that salary is discussed at interview. If for some reason the salary point is not made clear at interview it is advisable to accept the post on a provisional basis, subject to salary and contract. This will then ensure a written offer of the post is made detailing salary point, with the breakdown of how that has been worked out, and the terms of the contract of employment.

Conclusion

Market forces applied to the education service have had a serious effect on the conditions of service of schoolteachers and on their salaries. It inevitably means local variations within the national framework; sometimes this local interpretation at school level can work to the advantage of teachers, sometimes not. One recent test of this is the manner in which the terms of DfEE Circular 2/98 *Reducing the Bureaucratic Burden on Teachers* will be implemented in schools. The Secretary of State for Education and Employment David Blunkett has said, '[c]utting unnecessary burdens on teachers helps us to raise standards in schools, and that is our top priority' (DfEE 1998b, front cover). So conditions of service are about to change yet again, hopefully this time to the benefit of teachers. The profession needs the confidence to take control of its own destiny. Perhaps when the GTC is established in England and Wales we will witness the beginning of a professional evolution that will benefit future generations of teachers and consequently future generations of children. However, the role of the GTC will need to be seen in the context of an education system, which a number of commentators (e.g. Allen *et al.* 1999, Chitty 1998, Cole 1998, Grant 1998, Hatcher 1998) have suggested is witnessing burgeoning privatisation. In order to protect and advance the conditions of service of schoolteachers, a major role of the GTC should be to resist this trend.

Note

1. At the present time 'permanent' only becomes significant after an employee has worked for an employer for a continuous period of two years. For this reason, some full-time union officials use the term 'ongoing' rather than 'permanent'. However, this ruling is being challenged in the European courts. The outcome of the Seymour-Smith and Perez case may change the qualifying period to claim unfair dismissal.

Bibliography

Advisory, Conciliation and Arbitration Service (ACAS) (1998) *Code of Practice for Time Off for Trade Union Duties and Activities.* London: HMSO.

Allen, M., Cole, M. and Hatcher, R. (1999) *Business, Business, Business: the New Labour Agenda In Education.* London: Tufnell Press

Chitty, C. (1998) 'Education Action Zones: test-beds for privatisation?', *Forum* **40**(3), 79–81.

Cole, M. (1998) 'Globalization, Modernization and Competitiveness: a critique of the New Labour Project in Education', *International Studies in Sociology of Education* **8**(3).

Council of Local Education Authorities/Schoolteacher Committee (CLEA/ST) (1985) *Conditions of Service for Schoolteachers in England and Wales*, 2nd edn. (The Burgundy Book).

DES (1987) Teachers' Pay and Conditions Act. London: HMSO.

DES (1988) Education Reform Act. London: HMSO.

DES (1990) Circular Number 7/90. *Management of the School Day.* London: HMSO.

DfE (1991) Teachers' Pay and Conditions Act. London: HMSO.

DfEE (1998a) *Schoolteachers' Pay and Conditions Documents 1987–1998.* (The Blue Book) London: HMSO.

DfEE (1998b) Circular Number 2/98. *Reducing the Bureaucratic Burden on Teachers.* London: HMSO.

Grant, N. (1998) 'Wealth of Knowledge', *Socialist Teacher*, April.
Hatcher, R. (1998) 'Labour, Official School Improvement and Equality', *Journal of Educational Policy* **13**(4), 485–499.
Local Government Review [605] 1969. Barnes v Hampshire County Council.
Ministry of Health (1974) Health and Safety at Work Act. London: HMSO.
Mrs Atkinson v Ellis Guildford Comprehensive School and Nottinghamshire County Council.
Mrs Clay v English Martyrs School.
National Union of Teachers (NUT) (1987) *Salaries and Superannuation Report 1987*, 153–63. London: NUT.
National Union of Teachers (NUT) (1988) *Salaries and Superannuation Report 1988*, 135–44. London: NUT.
National Union of Teachers (NUT) (1995) *Research into the Issuing of Fixed Term and Temporary Contracts on a Full or Part-Time Basis With Particular Reference to Women*. London: NUT.
Wragg, E. C. *et al.* (1998) *Teacher Competence Project: Occasional Paper No. 2*. Exeter: University of Exeter.

Appendix 1

PART XII – Conditions of Employment of Teachers other than Head Teachers

Exercise of general professional duties

41 Subject to paragraph 23.5, 24.2 and 24.3, a teacher who is not a head teacher shall carry out the professional duties of a teacher as circumstances may require:

41.1 if he is employed as a teacher in a school, under reasonable direction of the head teacher of that school;

41.2 if he is employed by an authority on terms under which he is not assigned to any one school, under the reasonable direction of that authority and of the head teacher of any school in which he may for the time being be required to work as a teacher.

Exercise of particular duties

42.1 Subject to paragraph 23.5, 24.2 and 24.3, a teacher employed as a teacher (other than a head teacher) in a school shall perform, in accordance with any directions which may reasonably be given to him by the head teacher from time to time, such particular duties as may reasonably be assigned to him.

42.2 A teacher employed by an authority on terms such as those described in paragraph 41.2 shall perform, in accordance with any direction which may reasonably be given to him from time to time by the authority or by the head teacher of any school in which he may for the time being be required to work as a teacher, such particular duties as may be reasonably assigned to him.

Professional duties

43 Subject to paragraph 23.5. 24.2 and 24.3, the following duties shall be deemed to be included in the professional duties which a teacher (other than a head teacher) may be required to perform:

43.1 **Teaching:**
In each case having regard to the curriculum for the school:

43.1.1 Planning and preparing courses and lessons;

43.1.2 teaching, according to their educational needs, the pupils assigned to him, including the setting and marking of work to be carried out by the pupil in school and elsewhere

43.1.3 assessing, recording and reporting on the development, progress and attainment of pupils;

43.2 **Other activities:**

43.2.1 promoting the general progress and well being of individual pupils and of any class or group of pupils assigned to him;

43.2.2 providing guidance and advice to pupils on educational and social matters and on their further education and future careers, including information about sources of more expert advice on specific questions; making relevant records and reports;

43.2.3 making records of and reports on the personal and social needs of pupils;

43.2.4 communicating and consulting with the parents of pupils;

43.2.5 communicating and co-operating with persons or bodies outside the school; and

43.2.6 participating in meetings arranged for any of the purposes described above;

43.3 **Assessments and reports:**
providing or contributing to oral and written assessments, reports and references relating to individual pupils and groups of pupils;

43.4 **Appraisal:**
participating in arrangements made in accordance with the Education (School Teacher Appraisal) Regulations 1991 for the appraisal of his performance and that of other teachers;

43.5 **Review: Further training and development:**

43.5.1 reviewing from time to time his methods of teaching and programmes of work; and

43.5.2 participating in arrangements for his further training and professional development as a teacher;

43.6 **Educational methods:**
advising and co-operating with the headteacher and other teachers (or any one or more of them) on the preparation and development of courses of study, teaching materials, teaching programmes, methods of teaching and assessment and pastoral arrangements;

43.7 **Discipline, health and safety:**
maintaining good order and discipline among the pupils and safeguarding their health and safety both when they are authorised to be on the school premises and when they are engaged in authorised school activities elsewhere;

43.8 **Staff meetings:**
participating in meetings at the school which relate to the curriculum for the school or the administration or organisation of the school, including pastoral arrangements;

43.9 **Cover:**

43.9.1 Subject to paragraph 43.9.2, supervising and so far as practicable teaching any pupils whose teacher is not available to teach them:

43.9.2 Subject to the exceptions in paragraph 43.9.3, no teacher shall be required to provide such cover:

(a) after the teacher who is absent or otherwise not available has been so for three or more consecutive working days; or

(b) where the fact that the teacher would be absent or otherwise not available for a period exceeding three consecutive working days was known to the maintaining authority or, in the case of a grant maintained or grant maintained special school or a school which has a delegated budget and whose local management scheme delegates to the governing body the relevant responsibility for the provision of supply teachers, to the governing body for two or more working days before the absence commenced;

43.9.3 The exceptions are:

(a) he is a teacher employed wholly or mainly for the purpose of providing such cover ('a supply teacher'); or

(b) the authority or the governing body (as the case may be) have exhausted all reasonable means of providing a supply teacher to provide cover without success; or

(c) he is a full-time teacher at the school but has been assigned by the head teacher in the timetable to teach or carry out other specified duties (except cover) for less than 75 per cent of those hours in the week during which pupils are taught at the school;

43.10 **Public examinations:**

participating in arrangements for preparing pupils for public examinations and in assessing pupils for the purposes of such examinations; recording and reporting such assessments; and participating in arrangements for pupils' presentation for and supervision during such examinations;

43.11 **Management:**

43.11.1 contributing to the selection for appointment and professional development of other teachers and non-teaching staff, including the induction and assessment of new and probationary teachers;

43.11.2 co-ordinating or managing the work of other teachers; and

43.11.3 taking part as may be required of him in the review, development and management of activities relating to the curriculum, organisation and pastoral functions of the school;

43.12 **Administration:**

43.12.1 participating in administrative and organisational tasks related to such duties as are described above, including the management or supervision of persons providing support for the teachers in the school and the ordering and allocation of equipment and materials; and

43.12.2 attending assemblies, registering the attendance of pupils and supervising pupils, whether these duties are to be performed before, during or after school sessions.

Working time

44.1 The provisions of this paragraph shall not apply to deputy head teachers, advanced skills teachers or to teachers employed to teach part-time and are subject to paragraphs 23.5, 24.2 and 24.3.

44.2 A teacher employed full-time, other than in the circumstances described in paragraph 44.4, shall be available for work for 195 days in any school year, of which 190 days shall be days on which he may be required to teach pupils in addition to carrying out other duties; and those 195 days shall be specified by his employer or, if the employer so directs, by the head teacher.

44.3 Such a teacher shall be available to perform such duties at such times and such places as may be specified by the head teacher (or, where the teacher is not assigned to any one school, by his employer or the head teacher of any school in which he may for the time being be required to work as a teacher) for 1265 hours in any school year, those hours to be allocated reasonably throughout those days in the school year on which he is required to be available for work.

44.4 Paragraphs 44.2 and 44.3 do not apply to such a teacher employed wholly or mainly to teach or perform other duties in relation to pupils in a residential establishment.

44.5 Time spent in travelling to or from the place of work shall not count against the 1265 hours referred to in paragraphs 44.3

44.6 Such a teacher shall not be required under his contract as a teacher to undertake midday supervision, and shall be allowed a break of reasonable length either between school sessions or between the hours of 12 noon and 2.00pm.

44.7 Such a teacher shall, in addition to the requirements set out in paragraphs 44.2 and 44.3, work such additional hours as may be needed to enable him to discharge effectively his professional duties including, in particular, the marking of pupils' work, the writing of reports on pupils and the preparation of lessons, teaching materials and teaching programmes. The amount of time required for this purpose beyond the 1265 hours referred to in paragraph 44.3 and the times outside the 1265 specified hours at which duties shall be performed shall not be defined by the employer but shall depend upon the work needed to discharge the teacher's duties

Appendix 2

PART XI – Conditions of Employment of Advanced Skills Teachers

Professional duties

39. A teacher who is an advanced skills teacher, in addition to carrying out the professional duties of a teacher other than a head teacher (as described in Part XII) including those duties particularly assigned to him by the head teacher, may be required to carry out the following professional duties:

(a) participating in initial teacher training;
(b) participating in the mentoring of newly qualified teachers;
(c) advising other teachers on classroom organisation and teaching methods;

(d) producing high quality teaching materials;
(e) disseminating to other teachers materials relating to best practice and educational research;
(f) advising on the provision of in-service training;
(g) participating in the appraisal of other teachers;
(h) helping teachers who are experiencing difficulties;
(i) working with teachers from other schools, whether at the school of the advanced skills teacher, at that of the other teacher, in higher education institutions, at facilities of the LEA or elsewhere;
(j) producing high quality resources and materials, including video recordings of lessons, for dissemination in their own school and other schools.

Daily break

40. An advanced skills teacher shall be entitled to a break of reasonable length as near to the middle of each school day as is reasonably practicable.

Chapter 2

Teachers' legal liabilities and responsibilities

Jeff Nixon

In loco parentis

It is of paramount importance for teachers to be aware of the array of legislation that affects their work with pupils both inside and outside schools. The aim of this chapter is to provide a framework within which it will be possible to act sensibly and professionally with due regard to the law and teachers' responsibilities both in general and specifically.

Let us first look at the way in which the concept of teachers' responsibility towards pupils has changed in recent times. We are probably all aware of the infamous phrase 'in loco parentis', which for many years served as a convenient shorthand way of describing a multitude of circumstances where teachers found themselves responsible for the welfare and well-being of children. Teachers should act in place of the parent (now we would say 'parent/carer') and in doing so act wisely and prudently. The problem with this formulation is that the wise and prudent parent/carer who has a brood of 30 to 35 children does not in reality exist. That old Latin phrase is too set in the past to be meaningful. Today, a higher expectation of teachers is apparent; an expectation that they will do a better job than some notional parent/carer may do.

It is interesting to examine the words of Mr Justice Hilbery when he defined the responsibility of teachers towards a group of pupils. In posing the question, 'What has a reasonably careful parent to do?', his response appears entrenched in an age that has long disappeared.

> Supposing a boy of yours has some other little boys, who are friends of his, coming to tea on a Saturday afternoon and you see them all playing in the garden. Suppose your garden roller happened to be there. Would you consider you had been neglectful of your duty to the parents of those other boys because, for five minutes, you had gone into the house and two of them had managed to pull the roller over the third? Would you think that, in those circumstances you had failed to exercise reasonable supervision as a parent. These things have got to be treated as matters of common sense, not to put on [a teacher] any higher standard of care than that of

> a reasonable careful parent. If the boys were kept in cotton wool, some of them would choke themselves with it. They would manage to have accidents: we always did, members of the jury – we did not always have actions at law afterwards. You have to consider whether or not you would expect a head teacher to exercise such a degree of care that boys could never get into mischief. Has any reasonable parent yet succeeded in exercising such care as to prevent a boy getting into mischief and – if he did – what sort of boys should we produce? (Barrell and Partington 1985, pp. 438–9)

This example is a quaint illustration that demonstrates how much has changed in recent times. Any teacher who nipped to the staffroom, for whatever reason, for five minutes and left a class, where there was the potential for danger, would not be given much sympathy. If, in hoping to seek justification, this passage from Justice Hilbery was quoted, the teacher would not be taken seriously and would likely to be the subject of a disciplinary action even if nothing of any consequence actually happened in the unattended classroom.

To take another example, as parents/carers, we would expect that when pupils are taken out on a school journey they would, at the very least, be counted on to the coach before departure, and counted off and on the coach at any stopping points and upon arrival at the destination, that they would be counted on to the coach for the return to school, counted off and on at any stopping point, and counted off at the end of the journey. You might also expect that this mundane exercise would be carried out by more than one person. Parents/carers, and the public generally, would be horrified if no counting was done at all; but it does happen.

As parents/carers become more aware of their rights under the law and the prospect of more cases going to the courts for consideration increases, it is inevitable that the tests applied to assess cases will become more and more rigorous. It is important, therefore, to consider tests for negligence in very general terms. For an action for negligence to succeed, three factors must be present: first, the defendant must owe a duty of care; second, by either act or omission, the defendant must fail to provide the said duty of care; third, damage must have occurred to the party or parties bringing the action.

Teachers' duty of care

There are three elements to the concept of a teachers' duty of care: the common law aspect, the statutory consideration, and the contractual obligation (for a discussion of this last element, see Chapter 1, where the Blue Book, the Schoolteachers' Pay and Conditions Document, was outlined in some detail).

The 'common law duty' was highlighted in the Lyes *v* Middlesex County Council case in 1962 (Local Government Review 1962) where the 'standard of care' expected of a teacher was held to be that of a person exhibiting the responsible mental qualities of a prudent parent in the circumstances of the school, rather than the home. It has been acknowledged that a teacher's duty of care to individual pupils is influenced by the subject or the activity being taught, the age of the children, the available resources and the size of the class. This can be clarified further by adding the proviso that, even though others may disagree, if it can be shown that the teacher acted in accordance with the views of a reputable body of opinion within the profession, the duty of care will have been discharged. The definition of the 'common law' duty of care may become even more sharply focused as progress is made to reduce the size of classes and with the establishment of the General Teaching Council for England and Wales (GTC).

With respect to the 'statutory duty of care', the Children Act 1989, Section 3, sub section (5) defined the duty of care as doing 'what is reasonable in all circumstances of the case for the purpose of safeguarding and promoting the child's welfare'. Teachers who are entrusted with the care of children during the school day have this statutory duty. The Children Act stresses the paramountcy of the wishes and needs of the child, reflecting the law's current more child-focused approach. Rather than the old-fashioned idea that a child was owned by its parents and this parental authority of property rights was delegated to teachers during the school day, the child's ascertainable needs and wishes should be taken into account by the teacher and considered in the light of the child's age and level of understanding. The teacher needs to assess the risk of harm that could arise to a child in particular circumstances, and to consider the safeguarding of the child and the promotion of the child's welfare and interest. This approach is clearly much more complex than the simplistic doctrine of the child as the property of the parents and demonstrates again how outmoded the term 'in loco parentis' has become.

It should also be noted that head teachers are required by the Blue Book to carry out professional duties in accordance with the provisions of educational legislation, education orders and regulations, articles of government of the school, any applicable trust deed, any scheme of local management approved or imposed by the Secretary of State and any rules, regulations and policies laid down by the governing body under delegated powers or by the employing authority. In addition, a head teacher is also bound by the terms and conditions of any contract of employment, which means in totality that the head teacher is responsible for the internal organisation management and control of the school.

If the concept of the 'duty of care' appears to be a complicated matter when it refers to activities within the school, it becomes ever more complex when a teacher is engaged in leading or assisting with activities off the school site, such as educational visits, school outings or field trips. The law on negligence is particularly significant here; the legal liability of a teacher or head teacher for any injury which is sustained by a pupil on a school journey or excursion would be dependent upon the three tests for negligence outlined earlier. If a child suffered an injury as a direct result of some negligence or failure to fulfil the duty of care, the employer of the teacher or head teacher would be legally liable. This is because employers have vicarious liability for the negligence of employees at work. Consequently where legal claims arise following an accident to a pupil, and there is a suggestion of negligence on the part of the teacher, the claim will most likely be made against the LEA as the employer of the teacher or the governing body in the case of voluntary aided, grant-maintained schools, sixth-form colleges or independent schools, if the teacher was, at the time of the accident to the pupil or student, working in the course of employment. It is, however, possible for teachers to be fined (see Chapter 1).

The standard of care required of a teacher is that which, from an objective point of view, can reasonable be expected from teachers generally applying skill and awareness of children's problems, needs and susceptibilities. Under health and safety legislation the law expects a teacher to do everything that a parent/carer with care or concern for the safety and welfare of his or her own child to do, bearing in mind that being responsible for up to 20 pupils or students at a time in an out of school activity is very different from looking after a family. The legal duty of care expected of an individual teacher can best be summed up by saying it is that which a caring teaching profession would expect of itself.

In practice this means that a teacher must ensure supervision of pupils throughout the journey or visit according to professional standards and common sense. Reasonable steps must be taken to avoid exposing pupils to dangers which are foreseeable and beyond those which the particular pupils can reasonably be expected to cope. This does not imply constant 24-hour direct supervision, whilst away on a residential field trip. The need for direct supervision has to be assessed by reference to the risks involved in the activity being undertaken. It is not enough to merely give instructions. The possibility that these instructions may be challenged by one or more of the pupils or students has to be taken into account, together with the risks the pupils may encounter if instructions are disobeyed. Equally pupils' *individual* levels of understanding and responsibilities must be considered.

Where teachers believe that a journey or visit has not been adequately prepared or organised, they should not be expected to participate. It is important to note the terms in which the teacher's concern is expressed. If it is seen as a refusal to participate, in some circumstances this could be viewed as breach of contract or as an act of insubordination and could possibly lead to disciplinary procedures. The onus is on the teacher to demonstrate that there are proper professional and strategic reasons which give rise to the belief that there is a lack of preparation and organisation. Where the journey is one organised from within the school, responsibility for ensuring that proper preparation has been made and that proper supervision will be provided is ultimately that of the head teacher. Therefore it is the responsibility of head teachers to prohibit journeys and visits if they are not satisfied with the preparation and organisation.

Satisfying the duty of care absolves teachers from legal liability. However, sometimes accidents occur as a result of the fault of someone with no organising or supervising responsibility for the journey; for example the bus company used for the trip. Should, an accident occur where pupils and/or teachers sustain injury as a result of some defect in the vehicle, the bus company would of course be liable.

Some accidents are pure accidents, not reasonably foreseen and not the result of negligence on anyone's part; if no one is responsible then there can be no liabilities. Consequently liability goes with fault. In the case of a pure accident no one bears liability. Schools and LEAs will be covered in this eventuality by 'no-fault insurance'. Some LEAs act as loss adjusters for their own insurance procedures and settlement of a particular claim does not carry with it a notion of liability on the part of the LEA as employer.

The Health and Safety At Work Act 1974

The Health and Safety At Work Act 1974 is one of the major pieces of legislation of the 1970s. It was and still is 'enabling legislation' and, since the onset of more and more Directives from Europe, the whole health and safety arena has become more and more crowded with regulation, codes of practice and written recording of such matters as substances that are hazardous to health, dangerous occurrences and risk assessments. It would be impossible for teachers to be familiar with everything connected with the Act; it is far too extensive a field. However, certain elements of the legislation are very important for teachers, particularly Sections 7 and 8 of the Act. The main responsibility under the 1974 Act rests with the employer, who has to take reasonable care for the health and safety of employees and others who are on their premises. This includes not only the children, teachers and support staff, but also parents/carers and other visitors to the school; in particular those making deliveries.

However all employees have a duty under the Act to take reasonable care for the health and safety of themselves and others who may be affected by their acts or omissions at work. Consequently teachers have a duty to take reasonable care of both their own and their pupils' health and safety at school. The law also requires employees to act in a co-operative manner with respect to any guidance provided by the employer to assist in maintaining a safe working environment. For teachers, this means following carefully school-based or local education authority guidance on policy and procedure, and ensuring they are familiar with such practices. It means in practice that teachers should act with reasonable care at all times and apply good sense to everything they do, including not taking any unnecessary risks or doing anything that is potentially dangerous to themselves, the children and parents/carers who may be helping out either in school or on out of school activities. There is a duty on all employees to report any hazards and potentially dangerous incidents at work; teachers should make themselves familiar with the reporting and recording system in their school (e.g. the accident report book). There may also be a need to report certain types of accident to the Health and Safety Executive for possible investigation, consideration of prosecution and recommendations to be implemented to avoid a similar occurrence. Occupational injuries should also be reported to the local office of the Department of Social Security; delay in reporting such injuries could result in benefits being lost in the short and long term. To facilitate all this, each school should have a trained and well-informed Health and Safety representative. The unions do encourage members to take on such a role, and provide comprehensive training in the rights and responsibilities associated with such a role. However, the unions discourage members becoming Health and Safety *officers* as, under the Act, such individuals are much more liable legally for their acts and omissions; representatives are not liable for the things they do or do not do as representatives.

Health and Safety representatives' responsibilities are towards the trade union members they represent only and their job is to ensure that information is made available, accidents and the aftermath are properly recorded and acted upon, investigations are carried out, where appropriate, and inspections of the premises are undertaken on a regular basis (at least once a term in school time). It is important for health and safety representatives to encourage everyone to report even what might seem to be a minor matter that may simply require cleaning up, or a small inexpensive repair. Seemingly minor matters can cause serious accidents. The most frequently recorded accidents in schools involve slipping, tripping and falling; usually because a patch of wet or rubbish on the floor has not been cleared away. Teachers themselves can contribute to their own accidents; the most common problem tends to be piling up furniture, attempting to mount displays or to change broken light bulbs on wobbly chairs or wobbly tables. The first questions anyone investigating such accidents will ask are why did the teacher not use proper equipment and, with respect to the light bulb, why, when it is not her or his responsibility, was a teacher changing a light bulb in the first place?

Teachers who undertake particular specialist activities, such as the instruction or teaching of swimming, trampolining, canoeing and rock climbing, are required to hold particular qualifications. There may also be a requirement within the qualification to regularly update the skills required in order to continue teaching and supervising the activity. Should there be any doubt about the need for an extra qualification or the need for updating, teachers should not take on the activity until the appropriate professional body or association concerned has been consulted. The health, safety and welfare of children in the care of teachers is a fundamental requirement. Parents/carers entrust their children to the schools and to teachers in particular; they do not expect children to come to any harm there.

Discipline and detention

Since April 1998, LEAs have to have 'behaviour support plans', which incorporate a statement setting out arrangements for dealing with pupils with behavioural difficulties, including the help they are able to offer schools in dealing with such difficulties, and in generally promoting good discipline. These plans must be published. Since September 1998, governing bodies of LEA and GM schools must set out a framework for schools' discipline policies. This is to comply with Section 5 of the Education Act 1997. This means in practice that head teachers must draw up the school's discipline policy and make it known to pupils, parents/carers and staff at least once a year.

Schools will now have a legal right to detain a pupil after the end of a school session, without parental consent, as long as the school provides the parent/carer with at least 24 hours written notice. For this to be lawful, the head teacher must have made it known generally within the school and to have brought to the attention of parents/carers that detention as a sanction might be imposed. The detention must be imposed by the head teacher or other authorised teacher, and must be regarded as reasonable; in other words it must be seen as a proportionate punishment. Any special circumstances relevant to the particular pupil must be taken into account. This would include the pupil's age, special needs, religious requirements and travel arrangements. The time of year may also be a consideration in some cases. The 24 hours notice can be given to parents/carers by post, via the pupils or by fax.

Finally, with respect to fixed period exclusions, head teachers have the right to exclude pupils for fixed periods of up to 45 days per year; previously the fixed period was 15 days per term. In addition, the appeals procedure on pupil exclusion gives the school the right to be represented at appeal hearings. The committee considering the appeal must take account of the interests of other pupils and staff at the school before determining that a pupil should be reinstated. If the school's discipline policy contains specific examples of the sort of behaviour that may lead to exclusion, whether temporary or permanent, this will be important evidence for an appeal hearing to consider. This change in the law should see an end to those unfortunate situations where a school has permanently excluded a pupil, normally for violent behaviour, only to find that an appeal committee has determined that the pupil has the right to return. When this happens it often leads to the members of teaching unions in the school being balloted on their willingness to refuse to teach such a pupil. In a small number of cases this has led to some adverse publicity with a pupil's name being made known to the media, with some individuals using the situation for their own personal ends or for the organisation they represent. Making a particular child a cause célèbre is not the right approach, and the new provision will at least create a more balanced approach to the decision-making process. Confidentiality should be an important component.

Appropriate physical contact and restraint

DfEE Circular 10/95, *Protecting Children from Abuse* (DfEE 1995), provides guidance about physical contact with pupils or students. Appropriate points of that guidance have now been incorporated into Section 550A of the Education Act 1996, which is the subject of a later section of this chapter; however the relevant paragraphs of guidance are quoted here. These were drawn up after consultation with the teacher organisations.

> It is unnecessary and unrealistic to suggest that teachers should touch pupils only in emergencies. Particularly with younger pupils, touching them is inevitable and can give welcome reassurance to the child. However, teachers must bear in mind that even perfectly innocent actions can sometimes be misconstrued. Children may find being touched uncomfortable or distressing for a variety of reasons. It is important for teachers to be sensitive to a child's reaction to physical contact and to act appropriately. It is also important not to touch pupils, however casually, in ways or on parts of the body that might be considered indecent.
>
> Employers and senior staff have a responsibility to ensure that professional behaviour applies to relationships between staff and pupils or students, that all staff are clear about what constitutes appropriate behaviour and professional boundaries, and that those boundaries are maintained with the sensitive support and supervision required. That is important in all schools, but residential institutions need to be particularly mindful of this responsibility as do individuals in circumstances where there is one to one contact with pupils, for example, in the teaching of music or extra curricular activities.
>
> Schools may find it helpful to agree in consultation with the LEA or Area Child Protection Committee (ACPC) a code of conduct for staff to reduce the risk of allegations being made. Some LEAs have already drawn up such codes which are recommended to schools. Where a school agrees such a code, it should be made known to parents/carers to help avoid any misunderstandings.

Since 1998, provisions, contained in Section 4 of the Education Act 1996, have clarified the position in relation to the use of physical force by teachers. Under the headline, 'Teachers now allowed to hold, push and pull unruly pupils', the *Observer*'s education correspondent, Martin Bright, reported in the 26 July 1998 edition that the clarification was thought necessary because many teachers believed they were not allowed any contact of a physical nature. The General Secretary of the NUT, Doug McAvoy, was quoted as saying, 'This is sensible, straightforward advice that will help relieve the threats of legal action that hang over teaching staff.'

The relevant section of the Act, S550A, defines the powers of members of staff to restrain pupils or students. Staff can use such force as is reasonable in the circumstances for the purpose of preventing the pupil from doing or continuing to do any of the following:

(a) committing any offence;
(b) causing personal injury to or damage to the property of any person (including him or herself); or
(c) engaging in any behaviour prejudicial to the maintenance of good order and

discipline at the school or among any of its pupils, whether that behaviour occurs in a teaching session or elsewhere.

These circumstances apply where a member of staff of a school is:

(a) on the premises of the school; or
(b) elsewhere at a time when, as a member of staff, he or she has lawful control or charge of the pupil concerned. (DfE Circular 10/98, para. 10, p.4)

The use of corporal punishment is excepted from these provisions as it was abolished in the maintained sector in August 1986.

The term 'member of staff' is defined as any teacher who works at the school, and any other person who, with the authority of the head teacher, has lawful control or charge of pupils at the school. 'Offence' is qualified by the caveat that under a certain age a child may not be capable of committing an offence.[1] The interpretation of this section of the law, therefore, is open to conjecture; the initial assessment and judgement of the teacher and the subsequent course of action adopted will be critical in assessing whether the amount of force used is reasonable. This will also be dependent upon a number of variables such as the age and size of the pupil and how much the teacher knows about the pupil/student. Other variables may be relevant; for example, whether the pupil/student concerned suffers from any pre-existing medical condition that may or may not have been known to the member of staff concerned. Restraining, by use of physical force, a pupil/student who suffers from brittle bone disease, for example, may not be considered a reasonable option in the circumstances.

Before the implementation of the Act, force was allowed in an emergency only; where pupils placed themselves at risk of physical injury, where pupil actions placed others at risk of physical injury and where damage to property could be limited by the use of restraint, without endangering the physical safety of pupils, staff or members of the public. The new provisions make clear that teachers and other authorised members of staff are entitled to intervene in other, less extreme, situations.

There is no definition in the Act of what constitutes 'reasonable force'. The interpretation of this is crucial for teachers and others defending their actions. It must be emphasised that the use of any degree of force is unlawful if the particular circumstances do not warrant it. The degree of force should be in proportion to the circumstances and seriousness of the behaviour or consequences it is intended to prevent. The level and duration of the force used should be the minimum necessary to achieve the desired result, such as to restore safety.

In some circumstances it will, of course, be inadvisable for a teacher to intervene without help, particularly where a number of pupils are involved and where pupils are older and more physically mature. Unless this was considered, the teacher might be at risk of injury and clearly this should be avoided.

Although the new provisions do not specifically mention the failure to take appropriate action, in circumstances which merit the use of reasonable force, such failure could be regarded as seriously as over-reacting. This means that it is no longer possible to argue that it is a safer option for a member of staff to do nothing or to take very limited action, when to take some action would restore safety. As far as a teacher's duty of care is concerned, an omission can be significant if there were to be a subsequent claim for negligence. Having said that, a teacher would not be expected to intervene to restore safety, at all costs, to the personal safety of the teacher concerned. It is a matter for professional judgement that may need to stand up to detailed analysis and justification at a later time.

Since 1994, the DfEE has provided specific guidance on the physical restraint and education of children with emotional and behavioural difficulties (EBD) contained in Circular 9/94. Schools are required to have clear written policies on controls, restrictions and sanctions that can be used in dealing with EBD pupils/students and a positive approach is encouraged where intervention by teachers is based upon reward rather than punishment.

There is an acknowledgement in the circular, however, that difficulties in relation to EDB pupils are likely to be more severe and occur more frequently than with other children. Circular 9/94 advises:

> Physical contact and restraint should never be used in anger, and teachers should seek to avoid any injury to the child. They are not expected to restrain a child if by doing so they will put themselves at risk. Brief periods of withdrawal away from the point of conflict into a calmer environment may be more effective for an agitated child than holding or physical restraint. Parents with children in special schools should be told how restraint is being exercised. Children who require complex or repeated physical management should have a prescribed, written handling policy. Staff dealing with them should be trained in proper and safe methods of restraint (pp. 37, 38).
>
> The Department of Health has issued guidance entitled 'Permissible Forms of Control in Children's Residential Care' (April 1993). This guidance is designed to cover young people living in Children's Homes, rather than in schools, but offers positive and practical advice to staff on the care and control of young people in residential accommodation (p. 38).

Section 550A of the Education Act 1996 applies equally to EDB children.

The National Union of Teachers recommends that all incidents of restraint should be logged in a record book provided for that purpose and regularly monitored by a senior member of staff. The record should be contemporaneous and sufficiently detailed to help in any later investigation or complaint. It is advisable to inform parents/carers of any recorded incident. Since September 1998, all schools are required to have a behaviour policy which may well include guidance on the use of physical restraint involving touching, pushing, pulling and holding. Teachers will need to be made familiar with the school's policy and ensure they act within its terms at all times.

Training in methods of restraint may be considered appropriate for some staff and for certain types of school; however, the training provided should be appropriate and suitable people should be involved in its provision. A few years ago a residential special school that had encountered a number of students, mainly adolescent boys, exhibiting aggressive and challenging behaviour, brought in some prison officers on a training day to give instruction in physical restraint. The whole staff, teaching and support staff received the training. Afterwards the incidence of restraint increased dramatically and the injuries to students also gave cause for concern. Physical restraint and punishment almost became synonymous in the school and it is not surprising that shortly after an LEA inquiry into the school and its climate of indiscipline, it was recommended for closure

Sex, 'race' and disability discrimination

Under the Sex Discrimination Act 1975 and the Race Relations Act 1976, it is unlawful to discriminate against a person on grounds of sex or marital status, or on racial grounds. The latter includes 'race', colour, nationality, citizenship, ethnic or national origins. It is unlawful to discriminate against a person directly or indirectly.

Direct discrimination

Direct discrimination is where, in similar circumstances, a person is treated less favourably, because of his or her 'race' or sex than another person of the opposite sex or different 'race' would be treated. Direct discrimination takes many forms. In the treatment of pupils and students, for example, it may vary from crude remarks to subtle differences in assessment, expectation, provision and treatment. It may be unconscious or even well-meaning, however it is still unlawful. Racial or sexual harassment is also a form of direct discrimination. Rights exist on 'race' and sex discrimination when candidates apply for posts and during the interview and other selection processes. This means that short-listing and questions at interview must not contravene the legislation. The woman candidate who was asked at interview for the Head of Technology Department how she would deal with all the reactionary men who currently worked in the department suffered an incidence of sex discrimination on two counts: first, the terms of the question itself and second, the woman claimed that the question was discriminatory and sexist because the same question could not be put to a man and because it challenged her as a woman, rather than as a professional. She was the only candidate who was asked the question, all the other candidates being men (NUT 1991a, p. 25).

Indirect discrimination

Indirect discrimination is more complex. It occurs when a requirement or condition, although applied equally, is such that a considerably smaller proportion of a particular racial group or sex can comply with it and when this cannot be objectively justified. The phrase 'objectively justifiable' means in an educational context that the condition or requirement cannot be justifiable on educational or other grounds. It has to be a question of examining the facts and the reason for the objective justification put forward in each and every case. An example of this is a case that reached the House of Lords[2] and involved the requirement to wear a cap as part of a school uniform. Although applied equally to all pupils and students, it had the effect of excluding Sikh boys from a particular school and this was not justifiable on educational grounds and, therefore, constituted unlawful indirect racial discrimination.

In schools, discrimination is specifically unlawful with respect to the terms of admission. Schools must not refuse to admit pupils or to employ staff on grounds of 'race' or sex. In addition, any arrangement that does not afford pupils equal access to benefits, facilities or services is also unlawful. Finally, it is against the law to exclude pupils from school or to subject them to any other detriment on grounds of sex or 'race'. The law makes an exception for single-sex schools although in doing so, it stipulates that the facilities available should be no less favourable than those in any other school in a given LEA.

The Commission for Racial Equality and the Equal Opportunities Commission have both issued Codes of Practice on the elimination of discrimination and organisations such as the National Union of Teachers publish, from time to time, pamphlets and research findings on a variety of equal opportunities issues (see, for example, NUT 1988, 1989a, b, c, 1991a, b, 1992, 1995). Any complaints against schools or LEAs concerning discrimination can be made to the Secretary of State for Education and Employment or, if a legal redress is sought, one can go to the county court. Complaints by employees or potential employees can be brought, without any need for a qualifying period, to Employment Tribunals in cases that relate to sex and race discrimination.

The Disability Discrimination Act 1995

The Disability Discrimination Act (DDA), introduced in 1995, addresses discrimination in employment and in the provision of goods and services. It abolishes the employment quota of 3 per cent for disabled people established under the Disabled Persons (Employment) Act 1944. This quota system, whereby employers had to employ a minimum percentage of registered disabled people, was introduced towards the end of the Second World War when many service men and women were returning to the labour market and some had suffered disabling injuries during wartime service. The 1995 Act covers temporary and part-time staff as well as permanent and full-time staff.

Section 5 sub-section 1 of the Act states that 'an employer discriminates against a disabled person if, for any reason relating to their disability, the employer treats them less favourably than he treats or would treat others not having the disability and he cannot show that the treatment is justified.' (DDA 1995, cited in TUC 1996, p. 2)

Teachers need to be aware of this not only in relation to disabled pupils in their care and in the interests of fostering greater awareness on the part of all the children about the needs, perceptions and feelings of disabled people, but also in relation to the employment of disabled young people when they leave school and enter the world of work.

Moreover schools need to be regarded as places of work for disabled people (both children and adults) and the 'reasonable adjustments' section of the legislation is particularly relevant in this regard. Employers have a duty to make such reasonable adjustments to the workplace, work equipment or organisation of work where disabled employees or applicants need them because of their disability. Victimisation is also unlawful under the Act and employers must not take action against any person (disabled or not) who uses the provisions of the Act or appears as a witness at a tribunal hearing or gives evidence during an internal hearing.

A disability is defined as 'a physical or mental impairment which has a substantial and long term adverse effect on the ability to carry out normal day-to-day activities' (DDA 1995, cited in TUC 1996, p. 3). An impairment is one that has existed for 12 months or more, can reasonably be expected to last 12 months or more, or can reasonably be expected to last for the rest of a person's life. The impairment can be related to mobility, manual dexterity, physical coordination, continence, and the ability to lift, carry or move everyday objects. It can also be connected to speech, hearing or eyesight, memory, ability to concentrate, learn or understand. Some impairments will need medication or specific equipment. People with a learning or mental disability are covered by the DDA particularly when there is a substantial or long-term effect on the ability to carry out normal day to day activities.

The Act does not apply to employers with fewer than 20 employees, so the only schools which are not covered by the provisions are very small Church schools or very small grant-maintained schools where the governing body is the employer and the total number of employees who work at the school is less than twenty.

Employment discrimination under the terms of the Act takes place when an employer treats a disabled person less favourably than others for a reason which relates to the disability of the disabled person. If the reason for less favourable treatment was not related to the disability then that would prevent a claim being pursued. However, the reason does not have to be the disability itself; if it is *related* to the person's disability, it is discrimination. For example, refusing to appoint a teacher with a facial disfigurement, not because of the disfigurement, but because it is claimed children might be frightened or upset, would still count as discriminatory.

Probably the most controversial area in the definition of discrimination is the part which deals with justifiable discrimination. The Trades Union Congress is extremely unhappy about this concept and believes such discrimination can never be justified. As case law develops on this point and others, it may become clearer what this part of the legislation actually means in practice. In the meantime negotiation and agreements on good equal opportunities policies, procedures and practices will have to be sufficient safeguards against employers using this part of the legislation to abrogate their responsibilities.

The Act applies to disabled applicants for jobs as well as disabled employees. So the recruitment practices of governing bodies must be in keeping with the legislation. The selection of the best candidate must be based on an objective assessment of the candidate's ability to do the job and in many, if not all, cases the disability of any candidate will be irrelevant unless, of course, the 'reasonable adjustments' section of the legislation is relevant. Indeed this may only become applicable when an employer takes on an employee who is disabled in some way or an existing employee reports an impairment that has lasted 12 months or is expected to last 12 months or longer. Examples that are given about reasonable adjustments include making alterations to premises, reallocation of work, transfer to another job or site, changing a disabled person's working hours, permitting reasonable absence from work for rehabilitation, assessment or treatment, providing training, modifying or acquiring equipment or providing special instruction manuals, providing a reader or interpreter and, finally, providing a disabled person with supervision and guidance in fulfilling the requirements of the job (all these examples cover all employment, not just teaching).

There are a number of tests that may help in making a judgement about whether an adjustment is reasonable or not. First, any action must be effective by significantly reducing the disadvantage the disabled person would otherwise face. Second, the financial and other costs must be reasonable, given the resources of the organisation concerned and any action must be practicable for the employer in the specific circumstances. Last, consideration should be given to financial or other help that is available to the employer from outside agencies such as the Employment Service or charities. The Placement, Assessment and Counselling Teams (PACTS), a specialist branch of the Employment Service, may well provide advice at the local Job Centre.

The DDA is enforced by the employer's grievance procedure, and the Employment Tribunal system. Cases are beginning to be reported where disabled employees have successfully won several thousands of pounds in compensation, when tribunals have accepted that discrimination has occurred in terms of the provisions of the DDA. Much of the legislation is subject to interpretation, so teachers will need to seek advice and support in pursuing claims under the Act and will undoubtedly look to the unions for assistance with this as they do with other issues that relate to employment, conditions of service, educational and professional matters.

Conclusion

Becoming professional is one thing; remaining professional is another. The days when the acquiring of a certificate to teach for life (or up to 40 years) are gone. The rate of change is so rapid and dramatic that the student teachers educated in the 1990s may not be equipped to function effectively beyond the early years of the millennium unless, and this is the important part for Government to understand, time is made available and built into the system for serving teachers to be given the opportunity for extensive professional development, education and training. Examples of good practice are already up and running with courses like the 'Keeping In Touch with Teaching' schemes. These are normally run by LEAs and are open to any teacher who wishes to return to the profession after a break in service, usually following absence for family reasons. There are also many successful Returnees courses that LEAs and training institutions organise. Perhaps in order to prepare adequately for the future, we might look back to the recommendations of the James Report, written almost 30 years ago. This important analysis of teacher training and the needs of the profession suggested a regular system of sabbatical terms or years dependent upon length of service. For example, a teacher with seven years' experience could look forward to a year's sabbatical which could provide valuable time for retraining and battery recharging. Money spent on that rather than on the introduction of the 'advanced skills teacher', would target resources in a more constructive and supportive way for the teaching profession and bring to the education service a precise strategy to improve the overall performance of practitioners, ensure there was adequate time for professional thinking and development and provide a substantial boost to morale, as well as making the teaching profession more attractive to potential recruits. While it may be true that 'everyone remembers a good teacher', a system must be devised whereby good teachers are not burnt out in a short time-scale. The implementation of this recommendation of the James Report is long overdue.

Notes

1. The James Bulger murder case opened up a debate that is still continuing into the concept of the age of criminal responsibility; the interpretation of the law on this point is increasingly flexible with a tendency to allow each case to be judged on its own merits.
2. Mandla and Mandla v Lee and Park Grove Private School Limited. 1983 Industrial Relations Law Reports 109 HL.

Bibliography

Barrell, G. R. and Partington, J. A. (1985) *Teachers and The Law.* 6th edn. London: Methuen.
DES (1989) Children Act. London: HMSO.
DfE (1994) *Circular 9/94.* London: HMSO.
DfEE (1995) Circular 10/95 *Protecting Children from Abuse.* London: HMSO.
DfEE (1995) Disability Discrimination Act. London: HMSO.
DfEE (1996) Education Act. London: HMSO.
DfEE (1997) Education Act. London: HMSO.
DfEE (1998) Circular 4/98 *Requirements for Initial Teacher Training.* London: HMSO.
Home Office (1976) Race Relations Act. London: HMSO.
Home Office (1975) Sex Discrimination Act. London: HMSO.

James of Rusholme, Lord (1970) *Report of a Committee of Enquiry into Teacher Education and Training*. (The James Report). London: HMSO.

Local Government Review (1963). Lyes v Middlesex County Council.

Ministry of Health (1974) Health and Safety At Work Act. London: HMSO.

National Union of Teachers (NUT) (1988) *Towards Equality for Boys and Girls: Guidelines on Countering Sexism in Schools*. London: NUT.

National Union of Teachers (NUT) (1989a) *Job Sharing for Teachers: NUT Guidelines*. London: NUT.

National Union of Teachers (NUT) (1989b) *Anti-Racism in Education: Guidelines Towards a Whole School Policy*. London: NUT.

National Union of Teachers (NUT) (1989c) *Opening Doors: Encouraging Returners Into Teaching as a Career*. London: NUT.

National Union of Teachers (NUT) (1991a) *Fair and Equal – Union Guidelines for Promoting Equal Opportunities in the Appointment and Promotion of Teachers*, 2nd Report. London: NUT.

National Union of Teachers (NUT) (1991b) *Lesbians and Gays in Schools: An Issue for Every Teacher*. London: NUT.

National Union of Teachers (NUT) (1992) *Anti-Racist Curriculum Guidelines*. London: NUT.

National Union of Teachers (NUT) (1995) *Research into the Issuing of Fixed Term and Temporary Contracts on a Full or Part-Time Basis With Particular Reference to Women*. London: NUT.

Note. The document referred to does not have a specific title. It is all part of the NUT's occasional but ongoing analysis into the use of temporary and fixed-term contracts. The best title would be: A report of a national survey into teachers' contracts featuring an analysis of the issuing of fixed-term and temporary contracts on a full-time and part-time basis with particular reference to women teachers.

Trades Union Congress (TUC) (1996) *The Disability Discrimination Act, A TUC Guide*. TUC.

Chapter 3

Child protection

Dee Sweeney

Introduction

The teacher's primary job is to teach. Bearing in mind the increased pressure that teachers, over the years, have sustained, with for example the National Curriculum, it would be easy to understand that many might feel that child protection was an additional role, on a workload which is already at breaking point. However, as teachers, we should perhaps remember the broader definition of education.

The National Curriculum is not the whole school curriculum.

> The whole school curriculum entitles every pupil to a broad and balanced curriculum which:
> (a) promotes the spiritual, moral, cultural, mental and physical development of pupils at the school and of society; and
> (b) prepares such pupils for the opportunities, responsibilities and experiences of adult life.
>
> (Education Act 1996 section 351)

Children who are being abused or are 'in need' would be limited or unable to reach their full potential. So if we wish to fulfil our primary role, that is to 'educate' them, in the broadest sense, a prerequisite of this would be to ensure that they have a safe environment, both within school and outside.

Teachers *are* key players in child protection. Outside the home, teachers have more contact with children and young people than anyone else. Hence they are in a prime position to be able to detect child abuse or spot a child in need. Teachers have a major responsibility for the child's welfare.

However, particularly in cases of child protection, this role can sometimes be arduous, and place teachers in difficult situations and dilemmas: is it abuse? (when does bullying constitute abuse, when does the natural curiosity about sex between children become an abusive friendship). When, *or if*, to refer. Who do I tell? How will a referral effect my relationship with the family? How will the other agencies respond? Is it my role and what will the possible consequences be? Going hand in hand with these anxieties are the teacher's own personal feelings. They may have been abused themselves. They may know the alleged abuser. It may be a member of staff.

These concerns must be balanced by the fact that teachers have expertise in child development and due to the very nature of their work, they develop trusting relationships with children. Children so often turn to teachers when they need help or want to disclose an abusive situation. Many parents and carers trust schools more than other statutory agencies and so will approach them for help and guidance. Teachers and schools are therefore in an unique position to detect the first signs of abuse, changes in behaviour or a child 'in need'. Teachers and schools provide a pivotal point of contact for children and their families.

Child protection is an emotive, complex field and it would be difficult to overcome all the concerns of schools and teachers. Having a clear set of policies and procedures will provide teachers with a focus on child protection issues and will delineate their roles and responsibilities. Similarly it is useful to understand how schools and teachers fit into the 'whole picture' of child protection. Hence it is important to understand the main principles which underpin the welfare of children, the legal aspects and the role of other agencies.

After many well publicised public inquiries, such as the Maria Colwell inquiry in 1973 and the Cleveland inquiry in 1987, errors of judgement by all agencies were recognised. Cases like this highlighted the need for more formalised procedures, enhancing and developing a proactive inter-agency approach, a sharing of information and a coordinated, cooperative strategy. An outcome of these inquiries was the Children Act 1989 and the follow-up document '*Working Together' under the Children Act 1989: A guide to arrangements for inter-agency cooperation for the protection of children from abuse.*

Children Act 1989

The Children Act 1989 came into force on 14 October 1991. It provides the framework for the care and protection of children and clarifies issues such as parental responsibilities, the roles and accountability of professionals, and the rights of children. It also simplifies legal procedures. The Act applies both to private law (e.g. disputes related to divorce) and public law (e.g. children who are in need of help from a local authority).

Although all parts of the Act are concerned with the welfare of the child, Part V pays particular attention to the protection of children. The foundation stone of the Children Act 1989 (Section 1(1)) is that *the welfare of the child is paramount.* This applies for *all* agencies and at all stages, whether this be when there are suspicions, at the initial point of referral, during assessment or at court proceedings.

Legal framework

It is important for all professionals who work with children and young people to be aware of and understand the main points of the legal framework. Legislation places the primary responsibilities for the care and protection of abused children and children at risk of abuse on local authorities. Local authority social services under the Children Act have a statutory duty in relation to the welfare of children that includes:

> a responsibility to investigate reports of children suffering, or likely to suffer significant harm and to take appropriate action to safeguard or promote the child's welfare. (S47(1))
>
> 'Significant harm' is defined as:
>
> where the question of whether harm suffered by a child is significant turns on the child's health or development, his health or development shall be compared with that which could reasonably be expected of a similar child. (S31(10))

Local authorities also have a duty under Part III, paragraph 4 of the Children Act to:

> provide services to prevent children suffering ill treatment or neglect and to reduce the need to bring court proceedings.

Local authorities also have a general duty under Section 17 of the Children Act to:

> safeguard and promote the welfare of children in need and in so far as is consistent with that to promote their upbringing by their families.
>
> A child 'in need' is defined in S17(10) as:
>
> (a) he [sic] is unlikely to achieve or maintain, or have the opportunity of achieving or maintaining, a reasonable standard of health or development without the provision for him of services by a local authority under Part [Part III of the Children Act 1989];
> (b) his health or development is likely to be significantly impaired, or further impaired, without the provision for him of such services;
>
> or
>
> (c) he is disabled.

Although social services departments have the principle responsibility in relation to child care and protection, Section 27 of the Children Act clearly emphasises the duties of other agencies, including education in the support of children and families. This includes the planning and provision of services for a child and/or family.

Although schools rarely get involved in court procedures, except perhaps to act as a witness, it is useful to understand how the legal framework has changed since the Children Act came into effect. The procedure has been simplified and takes into consideration the feelings and needs of the child. The two most important concepts are: that there should be as little delay as possible by the court in deciding issues (as this could be prejudicial to the child's welfare); and the court has to be satisfied that it is better to make an Order than not to do so.

Children's rights

As the Children Act ethos is that the 'child's welfare is paramount', the act recognises that to fulfil this aim the rights of the child must be recognised and clarified. Children therefore have the following rights under Section1(3) of the Children Act:

- to be consulted about their wishes and feelings;
- to expect reasonable contact with their families;
- to be able, in some cases, to ask a court to reassess an order a lower court has made;
- to give or withhold consent to treatment (dependent on age and maturity of child);
- to give or withhold consent to be assessed (dependent on age and maturity of child);
- to have their religious persuasion, racial origin, cultural and linguistic background properly regarded;
- to have their own solicitor;
- to be kept informed by the local authority.

Parental rights and responsibilities

Another crucial principle of the Children Act is that instead of parents having 'rights over' children they instead have 'responsibilities for' their children. These responsibilities are defined by the Act (S3(1)) as:

> all the rights, duties, powers, responsibilities and authority that, by law, a parent has in relation to a child and his/her property.

These parental responsibilities are retained even if the child is being looked after by the local authority or is the subject of a court order. However, responsibility can be shared either with other person(s) and/or with the local authority.

The Act stresses that those who have responsibility for the child should work in partnership. However it is possible that an individual, with responsibility for the child, can act independently *but* only when it is compatible with any court order under the 1989 Act. The Children Act recognises that this 'responsibility' of the parent diminishes as the child matures.

The Act establishes the rights of the parents/carers. These are:

- the right to have a say in any decision-making concerning their child;
- the right to have their views heard in court cases involving their child;
- that their right as parents, for children being looked after by local authorities, are protected.

However, these rights must go hand in hand with their responsibility for the child. Rights and responsibility for a child are irrespective of whether or not the parents are married, or whether they are separated or divorced. This does not automatically apply to unmarried fathers, but they can acquire it if the child's mother agrees or by a court decision. These parental rights not only apply in possible child protection cases, but in the everyday life of the child. For example, a separated parent generally has the right to see a child's report, attend parent meetings, be part of educational decisions. On occasions this can be problematic for schools who often have to negotiate between the parties.

Working with children and families

An integral part of the Act (Section 1(3)) is a 'welfare checklist' which has to be taken into consideration in any court proceedings and should underpin all work conducted by professionals in the field of child protection. The issues to be taken into consideration are:

- the wishes and feelings of the child, subject to the child's age and understanding;
- the child's physical, emotional and educational needs;
- the likely effect on the child of any change in circumstances;
- the age, gender, background and relevant characteristics of the child;
- the parents' ability to meet the child's needs;
- any harm the child has suffered or is at risk of suffering;
- the court's powers under the Children Act.

These issues should be taken into consideration in conjunction with a sensitive approach to the culture and background of the child and family.

A concern sometimes voiced by teachers is that if they refer a case, the Social Services and Police will storm in – with blue flashing lights – to remove the child and split up the family. This fear is also common with children who are being abused; the child wants the abuse to stop but does not want the family to break up. Forced family break-up may have been the norm in the past but intrinsic to the Children Act is acknowledgement of the importance of families in the lives of children and to meet this need the Act incorporates the following:

- children are generally best brought up within their families wherever possible;
- there are many advantages for children in experiencing normal family life and every effort should be made to preserve the child's home and family links;
- aims to prevent unwarranted interference in family life;
- requires the local authority to provide services for children *and* families in need;
- promotes partnership between children, parents and local authorities.

The Act stresses the importance of a partnership between the child, parents and local authority, as this approach has proved to be more effective. The Department of Health research document, *Child protection: messages from research*

(Department of Health 1995) clearly emphasises that when a 'partnership' approach has been adopted there are less cases of re-abuse to children.

The matters covered so far in this chapter demonstrate the basis on which the Children Act should operate, thus allowing the views of children and parents to be heard, whilst providing a framework to protect children.

'Working Together' under the Children Act

The Guide '*Working Together' under the Children Act 1989* (Department of Health 1991, currently under review and likely to be reissued with revisions) was developed jointly by the Department of Health, the Home Office, the Department of Education and Science and the Welsh Office. It provides guidance for all agencies involved in child protection, based on the Children Act 1989, and findings from individual cases. The document stresses that to protect children 'all agencies need to co-operate with each other, they must be open minded, with a clear procedure for decisive, and if necessary quick action.'

Local procedures

The close working relationships between agencies, such as social services, the Police service, medical practitioners, schools, the National Society for the Prevention of Cruelty to Children (NSPCC) and others, needs to be supported by joint agency and management policies for child protection. The forum which develops, monitors and reviews child protection procedures are the Area Child Protection Committees (ACPC). All areas have an ACPC which consists of representatives from all key agencies, and includes an education officer and a head teacher.

An important task of the ACPC is the production of local inter agency 'Child protection procedures', which all agencies should follow. The ACPC child protection procedures provide a mechanism whereby, whenever one agency becomes concerned that a child may be at risk, it shares its information with other agencies. All teachers and schools should work within the parameters of the local ACPC child protection procedures.

They apply in all schools and it is essential that all teachers become familiar with them, especially the designated Child Protection Liaison Teacher at the school.

The outline of the ACPC procedures is shown in Figure 3.1. The stages which are of particular relevance to schools and teachers are:

1. **Recognition:** Teachers are in a key position to observe any signs.
2. **Referral:** Schools are one of the main agencies for referral.
3. **Consultation with other agencies:** Schools may be called upon for further information, so that social services can establish if there is a cause for concern.
4. **Child Protection Case Conference:** A conference would be arranged if, after an investigation, a cause of concern has been established (in line with Section 47 of the Children Act) and there is a need for a decision to be made regarding further action under the child protection procedures. Normally an

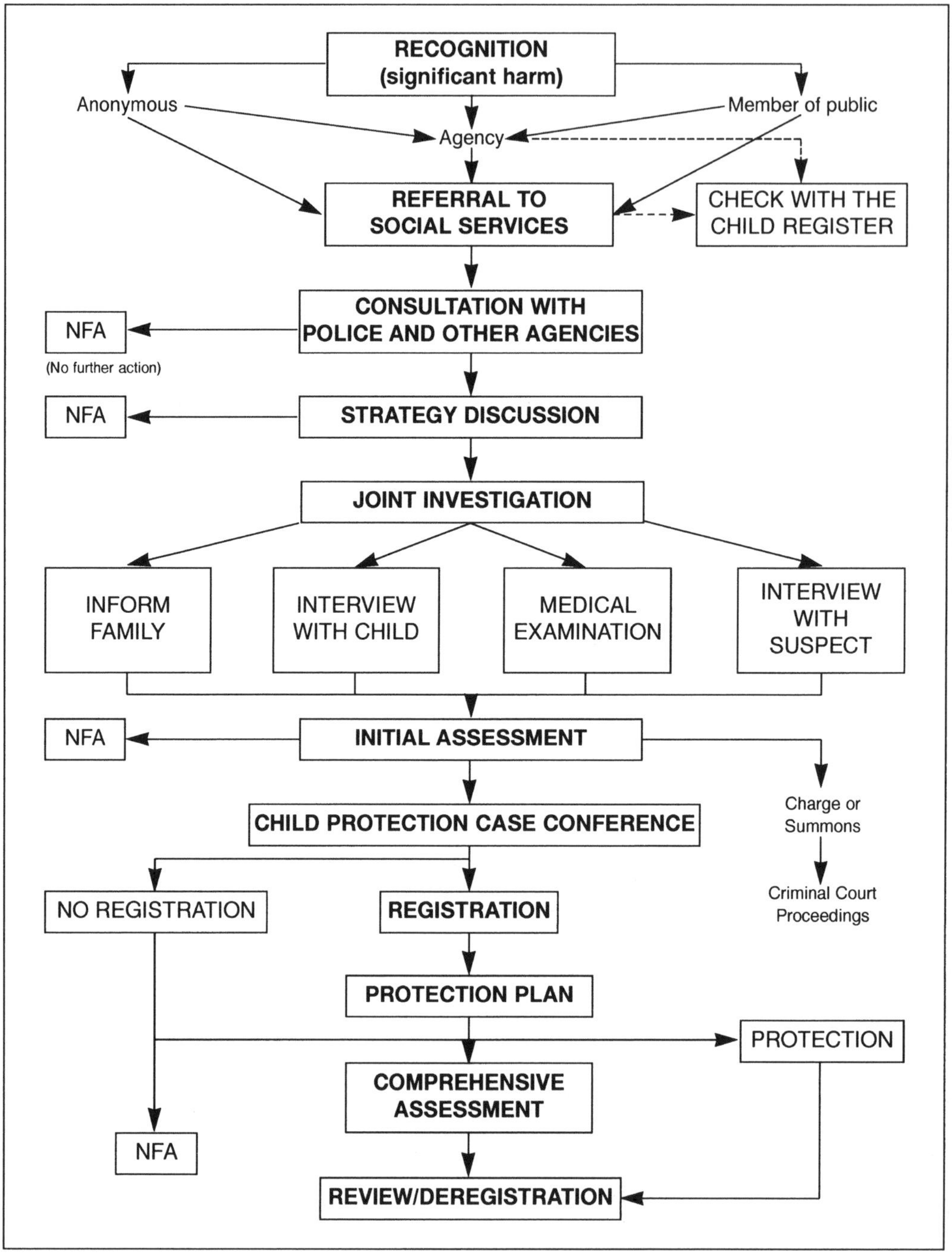

Figure 3.1 ACPC Child Protection Procedure

initial conference would be held within eight working days, except when there are specific reasons to delay.

The Child Protection Conference is central to child protection procedures and symbolises the inter-agency approach emphasised by statute and guidelines. The conference provides a forum where professionals and families (both parents/carers and children) can work in partnership, share views and relevant information, air concerns, analyse and determine the level of risks to the child and make recommendations for action.

The conference draws together staff from all the agencies who have specific responsibility regarding the welfare of children. This includes education, as well as social services, the Police and health, and any other staff who can offer any further relevant information or help (such as psychiatrists, interpreters). The school's representative may be the staff member involved in the case but generally is the Child Protection Liaison Teacher or head teacher. Anyone attending the conference should be thoroughly prepared and will normally have a written report covering past and present incidents of possible abuse. It must be stressed that in these reports the author *must* distinguish between *fact*, *observation*, *allegation* and *opinion*. Reports should also include the child's educational progress and achievements, attendance, behaviour, participation, relations with other children and, where appropriate, the child's appearance. If applicable, the report should also refer to the child's relations with his or her family and the family structure. Schools may have other written information relevant to the case, for example school reports. If an agency cannot be present it is expected that they would provide a report.

The conference is *not* a forum for a formal decision that a person has abused a child. This is a criminal offence and criminal offences are a matter for courts. The initial conference will concentrate on whether the child's name will be placed on the Child Protection Register. To place a child's name on the Register the conference must decide that there is, or there is a likelihood of *significant harm* to the child. To establish this, one of the following requirements needs to be satisfied:

(i) One or more identifiable incidents which have had an adverse affect on the child. These may be acts of commission or omission. These could include physical, sexual or emotional abuse, or physical neglect or a combination of these. It is important to identify specific occasions when incidents occurred, and to have available professional judgement about the extent to which further incidents are likely to occur.
(ii) The professionals judge that significant harm is expected, based on the findings of the investigation or on research evidence.

Other children, in the same household, can also be registered if they meet the above criteria.

All areas must have a Register, held by social services. The Register holds information relating to the children in the area who are considered to be suffering from, or likely to suffer significant harm and for whom there is a child protection plan. This Register is not a Register of children who have been abused but of children who have a child protection plan and for whom there are unresolved issues.

As education is one of the key agencies involved in child protection, teachers have access to this Register. This is a useful tool when there are concerns about a child and there is a need to find out whether the child is subject to an inter-agency child protection plan. All schools, however, should be notified, by social services, if any of their children are on the Child Protection Register.

Telephoning the holder of the register highlights a concern for that child which would be logged by social services. If a second enquiry is made about the same child (within two years) the second enquirer is referred to the first enquirer so further action can be taken.

If a child is placed on the Child Protection Register then:

(i) An agency (which has statutory powers – generally from social services or the National Society for the Prevention of Cruelty to Children) will be designated to take main responsibility for the child and a member of its staff will be the key worker for the child.
(ii) A Child Protection Plan is drawn up. The Child Protection Plan should include a comprehensive assessment. This is to facilitate a full understanding of the child and the family situation so that decisions about future action can be taken. The assessment should include contributions by all relevant agencies. The Plan will also clarify the roles of each agency, set a timetable for reviews and meetings, formalise contact arrangements with families if necessary, and strive towards establishing an effective dialogue between the child, the family and the agencies.

Although a social worker from the Social Services Department or the National Society for the Prevention of Cruelty to Children (NSPCC) will be the key worker, this does not imply that they would be the sole worker with the child or family. In fact, another agency may provide more face to face work with the family and child. The key worker, however, must fulfil the statutory responsibilities for their agency, which includes the development of a multi-agency, multi-disciplinary plan for the protection of the child and provide a focus for communication between the professionals involved. In addition the key worker must coordinate the inter-agency contributions to the assessment plan and review the case. The key worker also must ensure that parents and children are fully engaged and committed to the Child Protection Plan.

Teachers play an important role in the Child Protection Conference and subsequent conference protection plans and reviews. They can provide relevant information and insight to the child's background, needs and, if necessary, specific educational needs.The ACPC procedures come into play after a referral has been made. All schools should have a policy and procedure, with their own criteria for recording incidents, for reporting and for referral.

The role of teachers and schools in child protection

The important premise of the Children Act 1989; also emphasised in *Working Together*, is that the child's welfare is paramount. Therefore the school's first duty of care is to the child, not the parent or carer. However, this is not to imply that parents and carers do not play an important role, but to emphasise that when there may be a conflict of interests between parents or carers and the child, the child's needs and welfare must take priority.

As outlined in DfEE Circular 10/95 *Protecting Children from Abuse: the Role of the Education Service* (DfEE 1995), teachers and schools play a vital role in the recognition and referral of suspected child protection cases. Schools are however *not* an investigative or intervention agency, although they do have a duty to cooperate, share information and be an active member of the local child protection network.

Circular 10/95 states that all schools should have a designated Child Protection Liaison Teacher. In primary schools and smaller secondary schools this is often the head teacher, while in larger educational establishments a senior staff member undertakes this role. It is the role of the designated teacher to act as a focal point for all concerns that teaching and non-teaching staff may have concerning a child. In addition, the designated teacher must be fully conversant with LEA and ACPC procedures and policies, and liaise with these and other agencies.

Unless the abuse is very clear-cut, a disclosure for example, teachers often find themselves in a dilemma. Has this child been withdrawn for the last few months because her cat has died – or is it something else? That child seems to be getting a lot of bruises – is it abuse or is he learning to skateboard? One of the problems of making more people aware of child abuse, is that sometimes you may see abuse where there is not any. Although, it is better to be wrong than to leave a child in an abusive situation, one should always try to find out if there is a reasonable explanation, not connected with abuse, for any signs seen.

More often than not, child protection is about putting a jigsaw together, gathering information to ascertain what is actually going on. As stated earlier, although schools are not an investigative agency it is essential that they gather as much information as possible. So often as teachers we have 'gut' feelings. A child may behave slightly differently, play differently, just 'not be themselves'. Believe in your gut feelings; you know the child.

Internal procedures

All schools should formulate their own internal policies and procedures, consistent with those of the local ACPC and LEA. Those schools which have clear policies and procedures are generally the ones which identify possible cases of child protection more quickly, refer more effectively, provide the necessary information more succinctly and accurately, and thus create a mechanism which effectively protects children in their care.

The procedure outlined in Figure 3.2 is found in many schools. If there is a case of disclosure or it is deemed there is sufficient information or suspicion to indicate that the child is in significant harm or likely to be, the Child Protection Liaison Teacher will directly contact the Social Services.

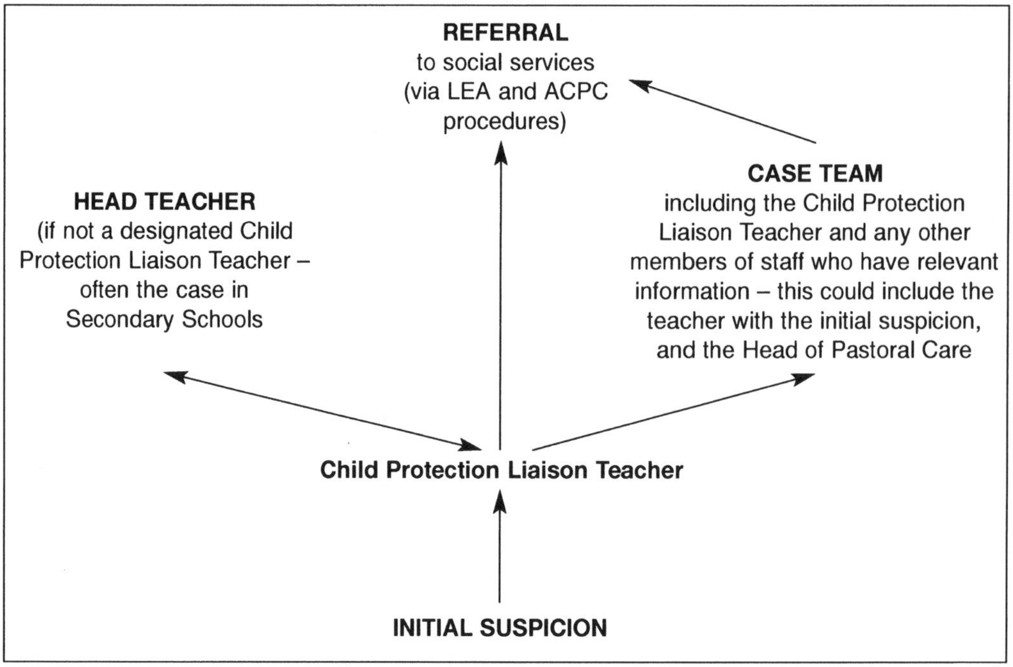

Figure 3.2 An example of a child protection school procedure

School's child protection procedures/policies are vital so that information can be gathered and a decision whether or not to contact Social Services can be made. As stated earlier, it is all about putting the jigsaw together.

Here are the different stages in more detail:

Initial suspicions

Suspicion may be expressed by anyone who is in contact with the school – a member of the teaching or non-teaching staff, a child, a parent, carer, or the lollipop person. Any suspicion, including 'gut' feelings, should be notified to the Child Protection Liaison Teacher. They should be recorded in writing, signed and dated. See Figure 3.3 for a record keeping format.

Another useful tool would be copies of the outline of a child's figure so that anyone who has seen any physical injuries can indicate the type of injury and where it occurred. Again, such a record should be dated and signed and attached to the main records.

These records are very important as they can:

(a) establish if there is a 'pattern' of suspicion (for example a child may be displaying disturbing behaviour every third week and this may coincide with

CHECKLIST FOR REPORTING SUSPECTED ABUSE

Name of Child____Age______________________

Any Special Factors (for example)
has the child any special needs
are there any known problems in the family (e.g. divorce, death)

Parent(s)/Carer(s) Name____

Home Address____

____

Telephone No:____

Are you reporting your own concerns or passing on those of somebody else? Give details.

Brief description of what has promoted your concerns: include dates, times, etc, of any specific incidents.

Any physical signs? Behaviour signs? Indirect signs?

Have you spoken to the child? If so, what was said?

Have you spoken to the parent(s)/carer(s)? If so, what was said?

Has anyone been alleged to be the abuser? If so, give details.

Have you consulted anyone else? If so, give details.

Name________________________Date____________Signature______________________

Figure 3.3 A format for recording child protection incidents

a particular event for the child, perhaps a visit of a parent or carer or other person);

(b) draw together information from a range of people, thereby helping to put the jigsaw together.

Both these points will help to determine whether there is a cause for concern and hence a need to notify the Social Services.

The records will provide the basis for reports going to a Child Protection Case Conference or to a court. Social Services need as much accurate information as possible to provide an effective service for the child. The records are strictly confidential, should be kept separately from other files on the child, and should be held in a secure place. Unlike other files to which parents/carers have access, child protection files are completely confidential and no parent/carer has a 'right' to see them. Similarly, if a teacher keeps a daily class record which includes incidences of child protection, all such incidences should be dated and signed and these records should remain confidential and secure.

All aspects of child protection are confidential and other people should only be notified of the case on a 'need to know' basis. It is very important that staff are very careful when discussing a case – it is so easy to be overheard.

If you are in doubt about whether something is important you should report to the Child Protection Liaison Teacher. There may be many other people who have concerns, but as yet there is nothing concrete – your suspicion may just be the piece of the jigsaw which completes the picture.

Child Protection Liaison Teacher and case teams

The Child Protection Liaison Teacher should be notified of any suspicions and kept informed of any further developments. However, it would be incongruous if this teacher were to take the sole responsibility in determining what should happen in cases of suspected child protection. As suggested in Figure 3.2, a small case team should be established from among staff (such as class teachers, Head of Pastoral Care) who have relevant information and who would together decide on further action. Decisions could include the following:

- one could ask the child for further information. For example, if a child is constantly covered in bruises, it may be abuse or it may be that he or she has started playing ice hockey. This request for information should not be phrased as a leading question and should be made in a friendly, unthreatening, unalarming manner: 'Hi, Chris those bruises look nasty – how did you get them?' How the child responds will inform further action. A record of one's findings should be made as soon as possible, signed and dated.
- One could talk to the parent(s) or carer(s). *No parent/carer should be approached if there are suspicions of sexual abuse or severe physical abuse.* In these cases 'tipping' off a potential abuser may endanger the child even more and/or the abuser will remove any evidence and intimidate the child.

Talking to parents/carers may also be in an informal manner. For example, when a parent or carer picks up their child from school: 'Mrs Brown, Sarah seems a bit down these days – is anything wrong?' Alternatively the case team may decide to talk to the parent/carer in a more formal manner. In these cases it is important that a senior colleague be present. This is to the benefit of the parent/carer and the teacher. It is essential to be open and honest with the parent/carer and explain why there are concerns. It is important to try to avoid losing your temper or sounding punitive. It should be explained that you have a duty as a teacher to report cases of suspected child abuse, and if applicable an explanation of the child protection procedures should be given. One should explain that the school may feel it necessary to contact Social Services and if this is so the parent/carer should be made aware that a social worker will be contacting them. By being 'up-front' with parents/carers there is more chance for the school to maintain an amicable relationship with the family. This will be very important for future working relationships.

Again, it is important to make a record of the meeting as soon as possible and sign and date it.

- One could take no immediate action but monitor the case carefully.
- One could informally liaise with other agencies. The school nurse, for example, is very useful if there is a need to establish that the child has no organic problems which could explain certain signs, such as brittle bone disease, Mongolian Blue Spot. Child Protection Liaison Teachers of other schools could be contacted to establish if there are similar concerns about the siblings of the child. Such contact might provide guidance and advice which make a referral to Social Services necessary.
- One could make a formal referral to Social Services.

Except for the decision to inform Social Services, the above points are not mutually exclusive. For example 'monitoring' may include making informal contacts, talking to the child and so on.

The Child Protection Liaison Teacher has responsibility for recording and collecting all information regarding the case, including the outcome of the case team meetings.

Referral to Social Services

Once it has been decided that a referral is to be made to Social Services, it is important that this happens as soon as possible. Any referral by telephone should be followed up by a letter, and a copy of this retained in the child's file. If a child is placed on the Child Protection Register then, as outlined in the DfEE Circular 10/95 (DfEE 1995) the school should 'alert either the child's key worker or the Education Welfare Officer when a pupil is absent or to any signs which suggest a deterioration in a pupil's home circumstances'.

Disclosure of abuse

As teachers are in position of trust, many children may feel confident to confide in them. It is therefore important to remember the following points:

- Never promise confidentiality. Most children will request this but explain to them that you cannot promise it. However, let them know exactly what you are going to do and who you are going to tell (the level of this explanation will be informed by the age and maturity of the child). This is in line with DfEE Circular 10/95
- Do not ask 'leading' questions, such as 'Did Uncle Jimmy do that to you?' or 'Did she touch you on your penis?' This is very important, especially if the case went to court.
- Once you have established a cause for concern, do not ask the child to retell his or her story.
- Although you may feel angry and disgusted, especially if the child has named an alleged abuser, try not to show your feelings. Remember that although the child wants the abuse to stop, the child may still love the alleged abuser.
- Remember to write down an account of the disclosure as soon as possible, sign and date it.

Allegations against members of staff

It is important that any allegations against a member of staff are dealt with in a similar manner to any other allegations. There are three possible investigative/referral agencies: social services, the NSPCC and the police, all of which have statutory responsibilities. At least one of these agencies shold be informed and all children and staff should be actively encouraged to report such incident. School procedures should include additional guidance regarding an allegation of abuse by a member of staff, such as the action to be taken if other members of staff feel that inappropriate or insufficient action has been taken.

Issues regarding the possible suspension of the member of staff have been discussed in Chapter 2, as have concerns surrounding, controlling and restraining pupils. Staff need to be aware of the recent legislation: Section 550A of the Education Act 1996: 'The Use of Force to Control or Restrain Pupils'.

Abuse by children or young people

A few years ago it seemed inconceivable that a mother would abuse their child. Regrettably it is now known that this does happen. Similarly, it is difficult to comprehend a child abusing another child. Sadly, we now know that this occurs. When handling a case where a child is the 'abuser' it is important to remember that it is highly likely that the 'abuser' has been or is being abused. In these cases the child protection procedures will be followed for both the victim and the alleged abuser.

Special needs

Special needs covers any child with a disability or children with Emotional and Behavioural Difficulties (EBD). All children with special needs, whether this is EBD and/or physical and/or mental disability, are often more vulnerable, and hence open to exploitation and abuse. This vulnerability may be due to the increased dependency children have on other people to undertake activities they are unable to do, this being especially true if the child has a mental or physical disability. A lack of self-esteem and confidence is a common thread among many children with special needs which again will make them more vulnerable to abuse.

Children with special needs are often difficult to work with and this can be particularly frustrating. Many children with EBD have been abused or come from problematic family environments. What teachers have to particularly bear in mind is *how* they deal with these children. For example a child who may have been neglected or comes from a family of 'high criticism and low warmth' may find it difficult to relate to people and may *seem* to lack the motivation to attempt anything which they deem to have a high risk of failure. Similarly a child who may have been sexually abused may shun away from any physical contact, irrespective of how well intended it is. Teachers working with these children must try to incorporate within their curriculum activities which might enhance the child's self-esteem, self-confidence and hence their self-image.

The curriculum

Self-esteem can be enhanced covertly within the National Curriculum subjects and overtly within the Personal, Social and Health Education component. In addition, as outlined in DfEE Circular 10/95:

> Schools can and many do play a part in the prevention of child abuse through the curriculum. Courses in personal and social education can help young people to develop more realistic attitudes towards the responsibilities of adult life, including parenthood. Some schools provide courses in practical child care skills, which may contribute towards better parenting.

Similarly, '*Working Together' under the Children Act* (Department of Health 1991) suggests that:

> schools have a role in preventing abuse . . . through the curriculum. They can help pupils and students to acquire relevant information, skills and attitudes both to resist abuse in their own lives and to prepare them for the responsibilities of their adult lives, including parenthood. Some schools include specific teaching about the risks of child abuse and how pupils can protect themselves, within their personal and social education programmes.

Whether to teach about abuse has always been a moot point. This is especially true when considering sexual abuse. However, perhaps we should consider the point raised by the British Council (1997), in their document *Children's rights: a national and international perspective*. This suggests that:

> the reason [for not teaching about child abuse] is that informing children of such things as sexual abuse will 'destroy their innocence' and that they are not

> sufficiently mature to comprehend such matters. It is suggested that it is the abuse itself which destroys innocence, teaching a child about rights which they have in relation to their own body is not a violation of innocence but a step towards empowerment.

Similarly the National Curriculum Council advises that the curriculum for children above the age of five years should include personal safety, including the development of necessary skills. The Council identifies three key dimensions, these being family life, sex and safety education, which should be incorporated within the curriculum.

Staff training

DfEE Circular 10/95 and '*Working Together' under the Children Act 1991* both emphasise the importance of training. An essential part of this training would be the consideration of what is meant by 'child abuse' and a 'child in need', with all staff being aware of possible signs of child abuse. Discussion on the definitions and signs of abuse are beyond the scope of this chapter. However, it would be pertinent to highlight the document *Child Protection: messages from research* (Department of Health 1995). This includes a discussion of the difficulty of defining child abuse and determining 'thresholds for intervention'. For example, if a culture advocates a more punitive parenting style (i.e. smacking), when might this be considered abusive or not, and who decides? If a parent/carer decides to walk around their home naked, could this be deemed to have negative long-lasting effects on their children.

If we wish to have a 'complete' child protection service, it is essential that everyone is aware of child abuse. This would include all members of staff within a school and within the wider community. The field of child protection is continually evolving, and staff require continual training to keep abreast of developments. Similarly, to provide an effective child protection service it is essential that agencies understand the parameters within which they work. A school, for example, might consider that a case is a matter of emergency, but social services may not assess it in a similar manner. This element of misunderstanding could lead to mistrust and irritation. These points demonstrate the need for inter-agency training, so that agencies develop trusting, cooperative networks, who understand each others' roles and boundaries.

Conclusion

Although the Children Act and '*Working Together' under the Children Act* are welcome steps in developing an effective child protection strategy, which promotes collaboration, cooperation and coordination, reality often is very different. We must not become complacent.

There are still inconsistencies and gaps in the protection of children across the United Kingdom and especially with respect to schooling. How can corporal punishment be against the law in state schools but not in private schools? Why is it against the law to strike an adult, but as long as there is 'reasonable justification' not against the law to strike a child. On 23 September 1998 the European Court found that the British law of allowing a parent/carer to cane their child (under the concept of 'reasonable chastisement') was against the European Convention on Human Rights. This will have a direct affect on British Law and it will be necessary for the Government to clarify which forms of punishment are 'justifiable' and to define the meaning of 'reasonable chastisement'. If we truly wish all children to have their own personal rights and be entitled to live in a safe environment then we need to iron out these anomalies.

Often, when people consider child protection, the image is of one person, or a group of people abusing a child. However, if we consider child abuse in its broadest definition, then society – both nationally and internationally – needs to examine how it treats children. Should the UK import cheap coal from Columbia – coal which is only cheap because children are used to mine it? Again, how can one justify buying World Cup footballs which have been manufactured using cheap child labour? Nearer to home we have a large population of children and young people, either sleeping on the streets or in inappropriate accommodation. Child protection is basically concerned with providing an environment where all children and young people are safe and have opportunity to fulfil their potential.

Bibliography

British Council (1997) *Children's rights: a national and international perspective*. London: British Council.

DfEE (1995) Circular 10/95 *Protecting Children from Abuse: the Role of the Education Services*. London: HMSO.

DfEE Education Act 1996 Sections 351 and 550A. London: HMSO.

Department of Health (1991) *'Working Together' under the Children Act 1989: A guide to arrangements for inter-agency co-operation for the protection of children from abuse*. London: HMSO.

Department of Health (1995) *Child Protection: messages from research*. London: HMSO.

Chapter 4

Critical pedagogy and the professional development of the NQT

David Taubman

Introduction

DfEE Circular 4/98, Annex A, Section D states that the newly qualified teacher (NQT) must 'understand the need to take responsibility for their own professional development and to keep up to date with research and developments in pedagogy and in the subjects they teach' (DfEE 1998a, p. 16). This chapter aims to address some of the issues involved in professional development and the NQT's responsibility for it. While the chapter addresses NQTs specifically, it is also relevant to teachers in general.

The chapter begins with a consideration of the notion of 'responsibility' with respect to professional development and some of the support mechanisms inside and outside of school which are intended to help foster such development in the NQT. Next, some pointers are given on ways of keeping abreast of recent developments in subject-specific research and educational theory. There then follows a discussion of pedagogy, in the course of which consideration is given to some of the variable factors determining pedagogic methodology, and some of its functions. The chapter concludes with a discussion of critical pedagogy, with respect to the work of Paulo Freire.

Responsibility for professional development

The NQT arrives at a first post, usually fresh from university, not sure of what to expect, and faced with piles of paperwork to digest. One may be keen to succeed and to develop a successful professional career, but where and how does one start?

School structures

In order to inform and support pedagogy, each school should have a 'Teaching and Learning' policy. This document, generally drafted by senior school management, should clearly outline pupil learning entitlements as well as teaching responsibilities. It should cover schemes of work, lesson planning and evaluation.

Since 1999, all new NQTs must undergo an induction year. To facilitate this, each NQT is assigned to a mentor. It is broadly expected that an experienced teacher will be appointed by the head teacher and trained to perform the role of advisor to the NQT, acting as a conduit by reporting back to line managers and/or senior management. The mentor will also keep the NQT informed of their progress, and offer general help and guidance as required. Mentors may also be responsible for observing the NQT's lessons, if this duty is not ascribed to line managers, as at present.

In addition, the mentor's role should be to discuss and clarify any problems or concerns of a pedagogic or professional-developmental nature, provide clear quick answers to simple problems and to discuss more complex issues, such as setting an agenda for research or action (e.g. on professional development or pedagogic practice).

A key aid to the NQT in developing professional practice and pedagogy is to watch other teachers. This can be done formally as part of in-service training (INSET) or it can be informal. Team teaching, a luxury in the present finanicial situation, enhances teaching and learning and offers pupils a good example of adults cooperating and working together, especially 'pluralist' or 'mixed' team teaching involving teachers of different age, sex, culture or ethnicity.

Whether done formally as INSET or informally, observation of other teachers must be a critical and analytic activity, evaluating the effectiveness of the pedagogy for that teacher, for that particular class, and for the school. To gain maximum benefit from observation, the lesson needs to be carefully analysed and it needs to be related to one's own practice. It should be remembered that what might seem good on the surface may be deeply flawed, while what seems bad practice may, in fact, not be so. Discussion about the lesson should be thorough and it should be collegial and not authoritarian or personal.

NQTs should also have the opportunity to have their own teaching observed by experienced colleagues and to receive prompt oral and written feedback and advice, as necessary and appropriate. Again, one would expect this to be collegial.

Finally, opportunities should also be provided for NQTs to share experiences with other NQTs in the school.

As far as the assessment of NQTs is concerned, this should be formative more than summative, especially in the first two terms. As such it can be viewed as another support mechanism for the NQT. The DfEE requires progress reports on a termly basis (with the final report focussing mainly on target setting), and the NQTs have the right to add their own comments to each report within fifteen days.

The target areas for assessment will be set by the NQT's Career Entry Profile (CEP). All NQTs bring with them from university a CEP showing their main educational interests (which may include some form of 'mission statement'), fields of specialism, some teaching materials and lesson plans. The CEP may also include observation notes as well as comments made while the student was on school placements. The CEP can contain anything the NQT considers relevant to his or her professional development. It should be referred to by the NQT at interview since it informs the school of the NQT's position and direction, showing his or her strengths and gaps in their knowledge and experience.

The CEP, in fact, forms the basis of the whole induction year. It enables the head and line manager, together with the NQT, to set targets for further development and it can serve as the basis for reviews of progress. It also has an important role beyond the induction year, in helping the teacher to take all key factors into account when mapping out a career path. If the CEP is used to form the targets for assessment, it must also contain the assessment criteria. As yet there is no final definition of assessment criteria, of what the legitimate expectations are to be, of what rights and obligations befall the NQT. The TTA is soon to issue exemplars for assessment to 'providers' (i.e. Departments of Education in institutions of Higher Education). The assessment criteria established by (or abstracted from) these exemplars will be disseminated by the DfEE to schools when plans for the induction year are concretised.

Finally, in our consideration of school structures involved with the NQT's professional development, we must turn to the factor of culture. Every school has a culture. Schools are living growing organisms, which change and adapt, which grow new parts and shed old ones; they have cycles, they have a 'spirit' (hopefully in line with their stated ethos), and they even have moods (depending on a range of factors). It is important that the NQT finds a post in a school with a culture commensurate with his or her own cultural reference points and work ethos; one too informal, for instance, would set the more formal teacher at a possible disadvantage; one too formal might have the same effect in the more informal teacher.

The culture of a school is an especially important factor for those not of the dominant culture, which, with respect to schools, tends to be white and middle class. For the Black NQT, especially the Black male (who can often be seen, subconsciously, as more of a 'threat' to WASP (White Anglo-Saxon Protestant) Alpha-Male dominated institutions than Black females), alienation from school culture (pupils and/or staff) can present obstacles to the smooth flowing of his or her other professional development, causing anything from a ripple to a tidal wave. In my experience the most important factor in 'fitting in' with the school culture is compatibility with colleagues in your department. This compatibility must be based on mutual understanding and respect of your professional qualities, as much as of your culture or ethnicity.

School culture depends on many factors: catchment area, staff profile and morale, the trend of examination results, structural factors like pastoral systems and parent involvement, the school environment and the presence or absence of a sixth-form. The NQT's first post should be taken with eyes wide open.

Before taking up any appointment, NQTs should be given the opportunity to visit the school, meet the head teacher and staff, and, where appropriate, the Head of Department and/or Head of Year, in order to find out all they need to know about the school.

So far we have looked at teaching and learning policies, mentoring, observing other teachers and being observed by them, sharing experiences with other NQTs, assessment, Career Entry Profiles and school cultures. This completes our overview of school structures supporting the pedagogic and professional development of the NQT. Before we consider the support-role of county and state, we will complete our picture of school structures by mentioning briefly the non-contact time stipulated for all NQTs.

The new induction year for NQTs includes a pre-existing structure of five non-contact days. Three of these five days must be ascribed to INSET and can include taking part in LEA (or other) courses, private study and observation in one's own or in other schools. The further two days should be used for general professional and pedagogic development.

LEA structures

The first point to make is that it may be the case that the Local Education Authority (LEA) has an 'induction day' when all NQTs in a given authority can meet. This can be a useful means of establishing long-lasting contact with those in the same situation as oneself.

LEAs should offer a wide range of courses, including some specifically for NQTs, as well as more general courses on pastoral, academic, classroom management, and professional development issues. Such courses are a valuable element of INSET during the NQT's aforementioned five prescribed non-contact days.

In addition, LEAs have their own Advisory and Inspection team, with subject-specialist teaching advisors who have good up to date knowledge of developments in teaching the subject as well as a broad understanding of catchment factors which may effect teaching and learning. They have the experiences of all the subject teachers in their Authority to call on. It is part of their job to disseminate to teachers new developments in their subject area.

NQTs should meet their local advisor in their first year. Before the meeting takes place, it is advisable to keep a note of appropriate questions as they arise. If, at any time, NQTs need advice of any sort from outside the school, the advisor is the first port of call. He or she will generally be pleased to help if possible, and, where necessary, will suggest appropriate action.

The relatively few support mechanisms at LEA level, compared with those at school level, does not diminish the important role local advisors can play in helping to empower the NQT to take effective control of their professional development.

State structures

The DfEE supports NQTs by instituting the induction year and by prescribing most of the school-based structures. Any specific queries about the detail of policy and entitlement for NQTs' professional development will generally be dealt with by the staff at the school.

The TTA, whose primary responsibility is the departments of education in the

Universities, is also involved in NQT assessment and in Career Entry Profiles from the student's days at university, through the vital induction year (for which it forms the developmental basis), and beyond (as described above).

The seemingly few state structures supporting NQTs belie their true significance. These state structures are what make the NQT experience what it is. They give it its structure and character (for a critical analysis of New Labour and education, see pp. vi–ix of this volume; see also Cole 1998 and Hatcher 1998)

Subject Associations

There are two other sources of information, which the NQT should tap in to in order to keep abreast of pedagogic and subject development in their chosen field.

First, there is a comprehensive range of subject Associations, at local and national levels, which NQTs can and should join (just ask colleagues or the local advisor). These Associations produce materials and publicise news, as well as organising occasional events. Altogether they pool human resources to the benefit of all involved, and much to the potential benefit of the NQT's professional and pedagogic development.

Academic journals

Second, the NQT, like all teachers, needs to read around his or her subject regularly in order to keep up to date with it and with developments in the teaching of it. There is a comprehensive range of journals to serve this purpose and NQTs would do well to familiarise themselves with them while at university, using the opportunity of the library to 'shop around' and find the journals which suit their needs and interests.

A list of some of the most useful UK education journals currently available form an Appendix at the end of this chapter.

So far in this chapter the main mechanisms for the professional development of the NQT in terms of school, LEA and national government structures, as well as in communities of discourse beyond these institutions have been considered. The responsibility of NQTs in managing their own professional development has been shown to be essential. The NQT in the induction year has an especially wide range of support structures designed to enable initial career orientation.

Of all the innovations involved in the new induction process, perhaps the single most significant new structure is the CEP, which forms the basis for the NQT's induction year, helping NQTs to focus on strengths and weaknesses and to set targets accordingly. For the values enshrined in the CEP to become part of schools' culture, the CEP must be seen as a practical token, aiming to establish professional development as the foremost tangible and quantifiable priority in teaching, a token intended to reinforce teachers' professional identity, self-image, or profile. It is also a means of quality control.

The role and nature of critical pedagogy

Having looked at the straightforward practicalities of maintaining pedagogic currency as a factor in professional development, we will now consider the fundamental role and nature of pedagogy, so that it is possible to see more clearly what it is we are supposed to be keeping up to date with and why. This is necessary as the rigours of PGCE and B.A (QTS) can sometimes blur the heart of teaching with 'information overload'. It is important, therefore, to establish a clear orientation at the outset.

Pedagogy is from the Greek *paidagogos*, meaning 'to lead a child'. In modern usage, it is generally accepted as a technical term for the 'science of teaching' (perhaps the term should more properly be 'pedagology'). However, it can be argued that pedagogy should include not only the component of technique, but also central moral and political components. Pedagogy is determined by the teacher's perception of the aims of education which in turn determine the nature (or sub-text) of the teacher–pupil–student relationship (or 'dialogue').

Pedagogy as 'the science of teaching' is holistic, in the sense that it must address the whole subject and object of teaching, giving a coherent model of the component parts. Pedagogy must make clear (by detailed critique – hence 'critical pedagogy') the grounds on which, as Smyth puts it, 'our means are related to our ends not in a [simply] technical, but rather in a moral and political way' (1996, p. 46).

Pedagogy is the DNA of teaching, the deep structure informing, guiding and constituting in all its parts the purposes and execution of teaching. 'Experiential critical pedagogy', of which Smyth is but one exponent (see also Boud and Miller (eds) 1996) focuses on the phenomenon of power and social justice. History and power are the dynamic base in which the superstructure of educational practice rests. They are respectively the context and the process behind teaching. Smyth's research points to the need for a greater emphasis on 'reflective teaching'. He identifies a four stage process, which, in the context of a political and moral process, involves the teacher *describing* their practice, *informing* or interpreting it, *confronting* or defining its cause and *reconstructing* or modifying it (1996, p. 50). Most British teachers do not engage at quite this radical level of pedagogic critique. Teachers' task-load is too heavy for us to engage in such lengthy process. However, the argument here is that we must.

In his provocatively entitled paper, 'Why no pedagogy in England', Simon (1995) points to a distinct lack of a pedagogic tradition here compared to other countries, characterising the English approach as a mesh of 'pragmatic' ideas formed in an academic context historically derived from public schools and Oxford and Cambridge and hence marked more by individualism than by clear and coherent educational purpose[1] (p. 10). In his classic manifesto of structuralist anthropology, Levi-Strauss distinguishes two forms of scientific enquiry, *ad hoc* 'bricolage', performed by generalists, on the one hand, and systematic science performed by specialists, on the other (1974, pp. 16–34). Although there are a great many specialist educationalists in England, the fact that the Government sets the education agenda without reference to an open and thorough pedagogic framework inclines us towards pedagogic 'bricolage'.

Reading Simon reminds one that a national curriculum without a basis in critical pedagogic discourse is rather like a government without a written constitution – open to the vagaries of political expediency and fashion. While, in other countries, teachers talk 'pedagogy', in England the buzz words are 'teaching and learning'. While teaching and learning are, of course, vital foci, indeed the primary bifurcation of the tree of education, the trunk is pedagogy.

The spectrum of teaching and learning covers too many aspects to discuss them all here. Two items are highlighted, namely 'pedagogical content knowledge' and the notion of the 'interactive–reactive continuum', for both have an important bearing on the type of pedagogic concerns noted above.

The term 'pedagogic content knowledge' was coined in the US by Schulman (1986). It refers to the interplay between specialist subject knowledge and teaching skills. It is knowing one's subject in such a way as to know how best to teach it, what Cooper and McIntyre call a 'transformative process' (1996a. p. 13) of turning content knowledge into teaching strategies. Cooper and McIntyre have identified four stages in this process: 'critical interpretation', 'representation', 'adaptation' and 'tailoring' (*ibid*). These translate into a reflective process of asking, 'What am I teaching and why?', 'How do I teach it and how else could I?', 'How can I tie the content in with the catchment and locale?' and 'How can I fit the content to the pupils in a given class?'. We can note that the first two stages involve critical evaluation of the fundamental pedagogic aims and processes, while the second two address the need to balance power in the classroom.

The 'interactive–reactive continuum' is based on what Cooper and McIntyre refer to as a 'transactional theory of teaching and learning' (1996b, p. 107), the idea being that pedagogic interaction in the classroom is essentially an exchange of power between teacher and pupil. They recommend 'a degree of teacher-regulated power sharing in classrooms' (1996a, p. 132). Pedagogic strategies range from 'transmission' (didactic depositing of information), through 'interactive' (plan-led), and 'reactive' (not led but 'negotiated' by teacher and pupils in an exchange of stimuli) to 'self-directed' learning (pupil led). Most teachers operate between interactive and reactive strategies, tending more to the former, and Cooper and McIntyre argue that we should shift the balance from interactive to reactive learning.

The relevance of this position to critical pedagogy relates to its focus on power and on the encouragement of pupil autonomy and critique, as opposed to passive acceptance.

There is no secret winning formula for optimal pedagogy. Rather, it is a process which is infinite and varied, unique to every teacher and fine-tuned to each class and individual at each learning encounter. The teacher must be sensitive to the needs of the moment and situation, and modify the 'pedagogic frequency' (but not the fundamental 'wavelength') as appropriate. For example, a science lesson in which the teacher adopts a pedagogic stance of co-investigator with the students might get out of hand with a lively Year 9 class in the last lesson on a Friday, so the teacher may take a firmer tone, or apply sanctions, but this should not involve the total abandonment of her or his co-investigative pedagogy. While it is good practice to use a variety of teaching and learning strategies with any given class over time, switching pedagogic bases (e.g. from 'enthusiastic co-investigator' to 'didactic authoritarian' within a lesson) can unsettle pupils or students. It can show weakness (inconsistency and fundamental uncertainty) in the teacher, and is likely to detract from effective learning.

In teaching, effective pedagogy is that which enables teaching and learning to develop without undue tension between competing educational objectives. It harmonises 'liberal education' (the pursuit of altruistic personal development) and 'exam' objectives, for instance. In developing your own pedagogic stance it should be remembered that, at root, to be an effective teacher one must have 'something to teach'. We should be clear about why we want to teach our subject and about how pupils can benefit from learning it, and we should be able to transmit that purpose to the pupils.

Effective pedagogy also consists in keeping up to date with developments in one's teaching subject, as well as in the teaching of it, helping to keep both teacher and pupils fresh and engaged, and helping to keep the subject itself fresh, engaging and relevant (i.e. bringing it to life). At a department level, this extends to keeping stocks up to date with new teaching materials too.

To sum up the argument so far, the school is an holistic organism generating increasing responsibility to all. The main responsibility of the NQT and of teachers in general is to teach well, and this can best be done with a clear set of pedagogic aims and up to date knowledge of subject, pedagogy and materials. This explains exactly why the DfEE document 4/98 includes the stated prescription regarding the NQT's responsibility for professional and pedagogic development, and it shows precisely how and why it is an important area of school life.

Critical pedagogy in action: the work of Paulo Freire

I would especially point all NQTs to the founding work of Paulo Freire, probably the single most significant and original educational thinker and practitioner this century (but see also Livingstone 1987, Giroux 1989, Taubman 1990, Giroux and McLaren 1994; Holland *et al.* 1995, McLaren 1995, Bernstein 1996, Kanpol 1997). Among his international activities, Freire organised national adult literacy campaigns in Brazil, Chile, Nicaragua, and Guinea Bissau. Following his release from prison in his native Brazil for his Jesuitical 'revolutionary' aims, he was appointed education consultant for the World Council Of Churches in Geneva.

It is Freire who really defined modern critical pedagogic theory. In recognition of this, he was awarded 26 honorary doctorates world-wide and 15 international awards, including the UNESCO award for education and peace in 1986. His work is as important today as when it was new. Why then is it not made readily available to student teachers and NQTs? His key texts *Pedagogy of the Oppressed*, and

Cultural Action For Freedom are not even in print in the UK any more.

If we are to take the teaching profession seriously, his work must feature on PGCE and B.A (QTS) reading lists. Can one imagine a national institute of physics ignoring or denying Einstein? The work of Freire represents critical pedagogy in its richest and most comprehensive, yet simplest and most direct, form.

For Freire, true education is a natural process of becoming increasingly human or 'orientated'. To be human is to be conscious of one's 'historical nature' as beings in and with the world (that is orientation), capable of transforming reality through 'praxis', a process of denouncement (of oppression/destructiveness) and announcement (of freedom/constructiveness) taking place in the pedagogic 'dialogue' between teacher and learner. The term 'articulation' (Taubman 1990) signifies the engagement in 'dialogue' at the same time as referring to the 'swing', 'realignment', or 'permutation', of meaning in the process of the transformation of reality.

For Freire, whatever subject is being taught, education is either oppressive or liberating; it cannot be neutral. If it denies the full participation of learners in selecting and defining the objects of learning; if it treats learners as empty vessels to be filled with knowledge; if it artificially separates the constituent parts of reality, causing confusion and disorientation, it is oppressive and denies human aspirations. If it is utopian, aiming to empower learners to transform the world towards a more sustainable and equitable reality, it is liberating. This is the essence of Freire's critical pedagogy.

So as we move towards the millennium, how does this rather philosophical theory relate to practice? Young people feel an ever-increasing sense of responsibility for the future, but this needs to be balanced by a matching sense of genuine empowerment. Critical pedagogy must be underpinned by a commitment to allow learners to actively engage (or as Freire might say 'to enter into a dialogue of cultural action') with the problems with which they are concerned and about which they are learning.

As a pupil I had refused to study because of the Atom Bomb and the threat of nuclear annihilation; it all seemed pointless. Now we are faced with the proliferation of chemical and biological weapons, rain forest and ozone depletion, mass pollution; 'ethnic cleansing' and genocide, AIDS, mass starvation, poverty, homelessness, mass global child abuse and a whole plethora of soul-shaking terrors confronting our young. Critical pedagogy aims to balance young people's sense of responsibility for this poisoned legacy, and to empower them to intervene in order to make a difference.

Hypothetically, a school which engaged in critical pedagogy might, in a given year, achieve the following. In Design and Technology, learners might develop alternative technologies (both hi- and low-tech) and suggest creative ways in which computers could be used to enhance global communication. The learners could be involved in selecting a campaign, either local or global, in which to get involved (agencies like Christian Aid and Oxfam are all set up for schools to use already). Active involvement with a development agency, in awareness-raising and in lobbying (e.g. for Sudan) might be established, as part of their humanities work.

This could extend, for example, to computer contact with a school in Sudan; a joint music and arts project with a Sudanese school, perhaps leading to an exhibition and a music CD for marketing; DT projects on well-digging and solar panel construction; mathematical problems and projections of statistics associated with Africa; fund raising to buy science equipment for Sudan and so on.

Critical pedagogy depends upon our human integrity informing our professional conduct. It requires us to 'get real' and break out of the tunnel vision, so apparent in many educational institutions. Critical pedagogy is not just about delivering knowledge, it is about being a whole teacher. Critical pedagogy is about the teacher and the learner, not just about teaching and learning.

Young people have their own sets of concerns and an education system or teaching ethos (pedagogy) which denies pupil and students' major fundamental concerns is inherently alienating.

What is required is a cultural regeneration for the millennium with the aim of inspiring a genuine sense of hope and purpose – based on the liberation of organic cultural action – for freedom, for pluralism, and for improvement in a society running on empty and in deep denial.

According to critical pedagogy, the teacher should ultimately act as co-participant with students in a mission to grow and improve. But our growth and improvement is always undermined by a lack of integrity if it takes place against the backdrop of a diminishing future which we ignore like a bailiff at the door.

How can the Government start to take on board such radically rational ideas? Do they not clash with the whole rationale of the education system? What about league tables and exams and discipline?

Effective pedagogy is that which enables teaching and learning to develop without undue tension between competing educational objectives. The balance is achievable. Some of the instances given in the hypothetical 'Sudan' school-year above (and some other very exciting events and developments) are actually underway at my school with great effect on morale and examination results in the relevant fields. I will leave the last word to Freire:

> As I write this, at seventy-five, I continue to feel young.... People are young or old...as a function of how they think of the world, the availability they have for curiously giving themselves to knowledge...as a function of the energy and hope they can put into starting over, especially if what they have done continues to embody their dream, an ethically valid and politically necessary dream. We are young or old to the extent that we tend to accept change...deeply living the plots presented to us by social experience and accepting the dramatic nature of reinventing the world and the pathways to youth...Pride and self-sufficiency make us old; only in humility can I be open to the life experience where I both help and am helped...The more youth educators possess, the more possible it will be for them to communicate with youth. The young can help educators maintain their youth while educators can help the young not lose theirs. Old as defined here cannot remake the world; that is up to youth. The ideal, however,

is to add, to the readiness of youth that the young possess, the collect *wisdom* of the old who have stayed young. (Freire 1998, pp. 72–3).

The satisfaction with which they stand before the students, the confidence with which they speak, the openness with which they listen, and the justice with which they address the students' problems, make the democratic educator a model. Their authority is affirmed without disrespect for freedom. It is affirmed for this very reason. Because they respect freedom they are respected. (p. 90)

And what could education do towards hope? Whatever the perspective through which we appreciate authentic educational practice... its process implies hope. Unhopeful educators contradict their practice. They are men and women without *address*, and without a destination. They are lost in history. (pp. 106–7)

Note

1. It would appear that the same is true for Scotland. The Scottish Consultative Council on the Curriculum (CCC) (1996) produced a paper, *Teaching and Effective Learning*, which demonstrates the pragmatism identified by Simon. The main text opens with a quote by Cedric Cunningham: 'Nothing is more practical in teaching than knowing how people learn.' We might add that nothing is more fundamental in education than considering why we teach.

Bibliography

Bernstein, B. (1996) *Pedagogy, Symbolic Control and Identity: Theory, Research And Critique*. London: Taylor & Francis.

Cole, M. (1998) 'Globalisation, modernisation and competitiveness: a critique of the New Labour Project in Education', *International Studies in Sociology of Education* **8**(3). p315–332.

Cooper, P. and McIntyre, D. (1996a) *Effective Teaching and Learning: Teachers' and Students' Perspectives*. Buckingham: Open University Press.

Cooper, P. and McIntyre, D. (1996b) 'The importance of power sharing in classroom learning', in Hughes, M. (ed.) *Teaching and Learning in Changing Times*. Oxford: Blackwell.

DfEE (1998a) Circular 4/98 *Teaching: High Status High Standards: Requirements for Courses of Initial Teacher Training*. London: DfEE.

DfEE (1998b) *Induction for New Teachers: A Consultation Document*. London: DfEE.

Freire, P. (1976) *Cultural Action For Freedom*. Harmondsworth: Penguin.

Freire, P. (1985) *Pedagogy of the Oppressed*. Harmondsworth: Penguin.

Freire, P. (1995) *Paulo Freire At The Institute*. London: Institute of Education.

Freire, P. (1998) *Pedagogy of the Heart*. NY: Continuing Publishing Company.

Giroux, H. A. (1989) *Schooling For Democracy: Critical Pedagogy In The Modern Age*. London: Routledge.

Giroux, H. A. and McLaren, P. (1994) *Between Borders: Pedagogy and the Politics of Cultural Studies*. London: Routledge.

Hatcher, R. (1998) 'Labour, official school improvement and equality', *Journal of Educational Policy* **13**(4), 485–499.

Holland, J. *et al.* (1995) *Debates and Issues in Feminist Research and Pedagogy.* Milton Keynes: Open University.

Kanpol, B. (1997) *Issues and Trends in Critical Pedagogy.* N.J.: Hampton Press.

Lévi-Strauss, C. (1974) *The Savage Mind.* London: Weidenfeld & Nicholson.

Livingstone, D. W. (1987) *Critical Pedagogy and Cultural Power.* Basingstoke: Macmillan.

McLaren, P. (1995) *Critical Pedagogy and Predatory Culture: Oppositional Politics in a Postmodern Era.* London: Routledge.

Simon, B. (1995) 'Why no pedagogy in England', in Moon, B. and Shelton Mayes, A. (eds) *Teaching and Learning in the Secondary School.* London: Routledge.

Schulman, L. (1986) 'Paradigms and research programmes in the study of teaching', in Wittrock M. (ed.) *Handbook of Research on Teaching.* London: MacMillan.

Scottish Consultative Council on the Curriculum (CCC) (1996) *Teaching and Effective Learning.*

Smyth, J. (1996) 'Developing socially critical educators', in Boud, D. and Miller, N. (eds) *Working with Experience: Animated Learning.* London: Routledge.

Taubman, D. (1990) 'Cultural Action for Pluralism: The Phenomenological Praxis of Myth in Education'. (D.Phil. thesis, University of Sussex).

Appendix: Some education journals

General education

A.C.E. Bulletin (Advisory Centre For Education)
Assessment In Education
British Educational Research Journal
British Journal of Curriculum and Assessment
British Journal of Educational Psychology
British Journal of Educational Studies
British Journal of Educational Technology
British Journal of Sociology of Education
Cambridge Journal of Education
Career Teacher (NASUWT teacher journal)
Comparative Education
Curriculum
Curriculum Journal
Education and Social Justice
Education Review (NUT)
Educational Action Research
Educational Studies
European Journal of Psychology of Education
Evaluation and Research in Education
Gender and Education
International Studies in Sociology of Education
Journal of Curriculum Studies
Journal of Education for Teaching
Journal of Education Policy
Journal of Educational Psychology (American Psychological Association)
Journal of Moral Education
Journal of Philosophy of Education
Management in Education
Multicultural Teaching
Oxford Review of Education
Pastoral Care in Education
Professional Development Today
Race, Ethnicity and Education
Research Papers in Education: Policy and Practice
Teacher (NUT)

Primary

Primary Geographer
Primary Maths and Science
Primary Science Review
Primary Teaching Studies

Design and Technology

Electronics Education
Art and Craft, Design and Technology

English

English and Media Magazine
English in Education
English Today
Reading
Use of English

Geography

Teaching Geography (produced by the Geographical Association)

History

Historian
Teaching History (produced by the Historical Association)

Languages

Language Learning Journal
Language Teaching
Links (produced by the Centre for Information on Language Teaching and Research)

Mathematics

Educational Studies in Mathematics
Mathematics in School
Mathematics in Teaching
Micromath (produced by the Association of Teachers of Mathematics)

Music

British Journal of Music Education
Music Teacher

Physical Education

British Journal of Physical Education
Bulletin of Physical Education
European Journal of Physical Education

RE

British Journal of Religious Education
RE Today

Science

Journal of Research in Science Teaching
School Science Review (produced by the Association for Science Education)
Education in Science

Special Needs

British Journal of Special Education
European Journal of Special Needs Education
Support for Learning (produced by the National Association for Special Educational Needs)

Chapter 5

School policies and practices: the teacher's role

James Parker

Introduction

For the newly qualified teacher commencing a first teaching post the discovery of the school handbook can be a daunting moment. Fear of the unknown is at its height and the self-confidence of even the most assured student is inevitably questioned: What will the classes you teach be like? Are you familiar with the schemes of work? Will you get on with the other members of staff? To be then faced with a bundle of policy documents relating to all aspects of school life can send the NQT reeling into despair. Do I have to actually *know* all of these policies? *What's the point?*

On the harsh and pragmatic level, the point is that you *do* have to! Circular 4/98 requires that all those attaining Qualified Teacher Status should understand their professional responsibilities, 'in relation to school policies and practices, including those concerned with pastoral and personal safety matters, including bullying.' (DfEE 1998, p. 16) Acting in accordance with your school's policies is a requirement of your job. This should not however be a cause for irritation or sleepless nights. As this chapter will outline, teaching is about more than simply the academic communication of knowledge. The school is a microcosm of society. Its joys and failures reflect the outside world in which we operate. Visits to only a handful of schools will immediately make apparent the fact that each school has a different 'feel' or 'culture'. When visiting schools you may immediately get a 'gut feeling'. This is no random psychological (or indeed psychic!) process: all schools have their own culture.

The culture of a school is not, hopefully, a random product. Each school should now have a set of aims and policies with which the new teacher should become familiar and, where these are effective, the environment of the school should be one that is conducive to every student achieving their own potential. During the inevitable difficult times as a teacher it is always valuable to remind oneself of the aims of schooling; why did you want to become a teacher? Only by reminding ourselves of this can schools, and teachers individually, seek to achieve these aims.

> At the heart of the work of a secondary school is enabling a child to become a student and more fully a person. (Marland and Rogers 1997, p. 1)

Your 'professional' responsibilities are not only the expectations placed upon *you* as a teacher by the hierarchy within which you operate, but also the expectations which we should all put upon *ourselves* to serve our students to the best of our abilities. We are in the business of building responsible adults from the raw material of children; to hide from such an important responsibility is to let down our own professional pride, but most importantly to let down those students who rely upon us for their future.

If we are to assume, as surely we must, that teachers understand the importance of their role in this process, why do we need to have a whole-school approach to such matters? Would the interests of students not be best served by a collection of individual professionals each exercising their own independence of thought and action; might an improvisational approach not serve to better educate students, providing role models for independent thought and action?

The Elton Report

A good starting point for the sceptic is the Elton Report (Elton 1989) – an accessible and stimulating read for all student teachers. The report was commissioned in response to media reports suggesting that physical attacks upon teachers were becoming commonplace in the nation's schools. The report concluded that, in fact, physical attacks on teachers were extremely rare, but that teachers *were* regularly facing minor disciplinary problems that were impairing their ability to teach in the way they would like.

During the week of the survey, 97 per cent of the respondents reported that 'talking out of turn' had been a problem in their classroom; 87 per cent reported 'work avoidance'; 86 per cent 'students hindering others in the class'; 82 per cent said that students arriving late to lessons had caused disturbance. In fact only 1.7 per cent reported that they had experienced actual 'physical aggression' in the classroom. (p. 239)

These figures were reflected in the wider school environment, with 93 per cent of teachers reporting 'lack of concern for others', and 90 per cent 'unruliness outside of the classroom'. Only 1.1 per cent reported any physical aggression in the week of the survey.

Clearly physical aggression is a very serious issue, to which Elton responded accordingly, but on the whole it did appear that most teachers were reporting that most of the time, minor disciplinary problems were occurring in the nation's classrooms, across a variety of schools in a cross-section of communities. Teachers were most concerned with, 'the cumulative effects of disruption to their lessons caused by relatively trivial but persistent behaviour' (p. 8) Apart from the educational drawbacks of such problems this was clearly contributing to a great deal of stress on teachers.

Was this worse than in the past? In fact we have no way of knowing, because no such previous research had been commissioned. Glynn is sceptical:

> The increasing subordination of the young is a perennial theme in western culture, a theme which is closely related to the wider myth of social disintegration that conservative writers have held from at least the seventeenth century. (in Wheldall, 1992, p. 21)

From viewing the apparent anarchy and slothfulness of students, and adolescents in particular, observers have always perceived society to be on its last legs. It is worth bearing in mind that William Golding's classic *Lord of the Flies*, and its cynicism regarding the ability of youth to find its own sense of order, was in itself a reaction to his own teaching experiences in the USA in the 1940s. Further food for thought are D. H. Lawrence's *The Rainbow* (written by another disillusioned teacher!) and the classic *The Blackboard Jungle*, an American film from the 1950s which should be compulsive viewing for all student teachers.

Growing media reports of unruliness in the classroom were perhaps not entirely unconnected to the phasing out of corporal punishment in the 1980s. It is difficult to accurately gauge popular opinion about how children should be educated in behaviour but, as Marland points out:

> There is a populist tendency in the country to think that 'good behaviour' comes merely from 'good discipline' and that ' discipline' is a matter of how hard you tell them off and clobber them after the event. (Marland 1994, p. 32)

It is reassuring, therefore, that in the face of this moral and political climate Elton's recommendations, based upon consultations with teachers, were far from the philosophy of the lynch-mob. Elton was not alone amongst commentators when he noted that the abandonment of the cane had provided a fresh opportunity to review the way in which schools 'controlled' discipline. The opportunity, or necessity, had arrived to produce a new learning environment where discipline was 'created' rather than imposed; from a *reactive* to a *proactive* response.

Although some older teachers did express concern about the end of corporal punishment, it would seem that the systems created in the new school world have been found to be more successful by those at the chalk-face than the brutality of the creaking control mechanism of old. One tutor reported that,

> It took a while to get used to new ways of thinking and to dealing with youngsters in a way which seemed soft, but we have now minimised the problems and the reduction in the number of serious incidents within a better climate has paid off. (Elliott 1991, p. 166)

Most importantly for those considering the professional nature of the job they intend to do is to understand that the more positive cultures which have been aimed for since Elton do rely to a large extent on a solid foundation of aims and policies. To reiterate, how can we know if we are achieving our targets if we have never defined what those targets are?

One of Elton's central recommendations was that each school should seek to draw up a whole-school policy on discipline, with the aim of creating, 'a school community in which pupils do not begin to consider behaving in such a way'. Indeed, it is now a legal requirement for schools to have a discipline policy and for LEAs to have a behaviour support plan. Elton argued that the most effective schools were those that have created a positive atmosphere based on a sense of community and shared values. He also emphasised the need for 'collective responsibility' amongst staff. The school either moved ahead as a team or it would go nowhere. (Elton 1989, p. 166)

Elton recommended that any policy that was to be successful in creating a safe and caring school culture had to be one that was acceptable to both the community as a whole and the staff in particular; it was the teachers who had the crucial role of implementing policies throughout the school day. Without a democratic 'rooting down' of policies within the staff-room culture, it was unrealistic to expect teachers to be either familiar with, or in favour of, what could be potentially seen as an irrelevance.

The emphasis was henceforth to be on attempting to build schools where students felt safe and secure. Attempts to encourage learning would be impeded on all levels if that learning was not taking place in a genuinely caring environment.

Pastoral care

With schools seeking to establish logical and effective frameworks for providing such an environment for students, many different paths have inevitably been trod. All have relied to a large extent, however, on their perceptions of the role of pastoral care in the school system. Many commentators have argued that many schools have in fact followed too strictly a 'pastoral corridor', separating this aim from all other aspects of school life. The very nature of pastoral care produces the need for lines of management and a clear delineation of roles and responsibility; in many cases this has compounded the problem, particularly in secondary schools. Pastoral matters have often been seen as a separate arena to academic achievement, yet the government's own advice has been that 'personal and social development and responsibility are intrinsic to the nature of education' (HMI 1989, p. 1)

The comprehensive system is one that was created in order to facilitate universal entitlement to education. Yet until recently classroom teachers were able to receive little or no information about the academic and personal background of the children they taught. Whilst it may, arguably, be healthy to avoid pre-judging students, in the world of the modern classroom and with the need for differentiation to enable all students to access the curriculum, it seems bewildering that for so long so little information was passed on. If a teacher does not 'know' her or his students – if a teacher has formed no human relationship whatsoever with her or his students – then the teaching and learning process will be fundamentally flawed.

> There can be no pastoral/academic split; there is rarely any curricula reality unless there is reciprocity between teacher and learner and where there is reciprocity – wherever there is human relationship – then there is 'pastoral' work. (Marland 1974, p. 4)

Under the Code of Practice (DfEE 1994), it is now one of the professional responsibilities of teachers that they do have a file on each of the classes they teach, informing their teaching of the different learning abilities, problems and achievements of the individual students within their class. To not do so would again be a professional failing in every sense of the word 'professional'.

Fostering a caring environment in our schools cannot happen by simply producing documents of intention. Pastoral systems and mechanisms are the route by which schools seek to ensure that the greatest concern is shown for the education of the whole person, and that the individual student is not an anonymous product in a faceless education factory. In fact, as has been outlined, any school that is not human in its approach to recognising individuals will inevitably be failing in any wider sense of the term 'education'.

Different schools have different systems in place, as a response to the perceived circumstances within which that school finds itself operating and as reflection of the educational and cultural aims of the staff, parents and governors within that whole-school community.

Within primary education the class teacher's pastoral role is clear, being directly responsible for all aspects of the child's personal, social and academic development and that responsibility being clearly understood by child, parents and teachers. The greater amount of time that the primary teacher is with individual students can enable the strengthening of the relationship between student and teacher, as well as providing strong opportunities for the teacher to monitor social interaction between students. This enables both direct intervention by the teacher to address problems within the group, as well as providing the opportunity for the teacher to raise and tackle social problems that have arisen during the day, week or month, with the group as a whole.

The promotion and development of Jenny Mosley's 'circle-time' has been a prominent success in fostering better relationships within groups and schools as a whole. In circle-time, classroom and playground problems can be addressed in a clearly structured and non-pressurised manner. The class teacher is the director of circle-time, but the clear rules (such as 'no names' and no talking without holding the 'talking Ted' or similar object) enable students to raise issues and gain peer support over matters that have been causing them distress. For example a child who is feeling isolated in the playground, or who feels scared of another student, can raise the issue within the circle. The peer-group can then suggest how the student might best address this problem. A crucial component of circle-time is that in this pastoral support system, it is the *student* who is being empowered to deal with situations, rather than simply becoming the passive recipient of pastoral care by the school system. The building of self-esteem is a far more effective tool in enabling students to handle problems than any amount of written documentation. As one teacher responded:

> Circle time can empower children who feel that they are in situations they have no control over, when they receive the advice or support of other circle members. (Mosley 1993, p. 24)

The whole-school's 'Golden Rules' are clearly displayed, understood and referred to in each primary school following Mosley' programme. Rules such as 'be kind' and 'listen to other people' not only come from the children, but they are also the central focus of circle-time.

There are clear lessons for secondary education in this field of student empowerment. The nature of secondary schools perhaps inevitably produces a less tightly focused pastoral atmosphere. Most secondary schools now have a pastoral system that is structured on a year group and tutor group basis. Within this structure the Head of Year provides the essential link in the chain between the school's management team (the Head and Deputies) and the individual student. A Year-structured system provides the benefits of a shared experience with approximately 30 peers as progress through the various phases of secondary education is made. It also has the benefit of enabling the clear addressing of personal and social issues relevant to groups of students of the same age. On an administrational basis it also has clear benefits in terms of communication.

Not all schools operate on a Year-based pastoral system. There are vertically structured systems operating through 'House' systems. In such systems a Head of House carries out a role similar to the Head of Year, but tutor groups are of mixed age. Having myself experienced such a system, I certainly feel that the personal and social advantages of such a structure are strong.

Each year approximately eight new Year 8 students are blended into an already established tutor group. Such an arrangement facilitates the building of a strong and caring 'family' ethos within the group, particularly where the new Year 9s, 10s, and 11s are encouraged to look after the new arrivals from local Middle Schools. Surprisingly warm, nurturing, relationships can develop from the most apparently unlikely combinations. The sight of the shyest, quietest Year 8 girls being shepherded around the school site at lunch time by a Year 11 girl, who many teachers have found to be an extremely 'difficult' student, has been a heartening experience. The benefits for both students have been manifestly clear in terms of each one's personal and social development.

As a tutor in such a system I have found that the relationships forged with older tutees have often been enough in themselves to educate some students into 'the family'. I am reminded of a particular gamble I took with a Year 9 student, new to the school. His reaction to me had been aggressive and defensive from the start, resulting from a history of personal and social problems. Close to the end of my tether on a rainy Friday lunch time, and in response to an outburst from the tutee aimed my way, I called in a Year 10 tutee, popular with his peers but certainly with behavioural problems of his own. I left the two together and asked the elder to 'have a word' with my Year 9 student and to explain 'how things worked' between me and the tutor group. After a few quiet words between them (I listened in, naturally!) the Year 9's attitude changed towards me overnight. Whilst problems remained, he subsequently put a degree of trust in me that no amount of time and energy from me as 'a teacher' could have drawn out. As Mosley's work has proven, peer pressure is an enormous influence on adolescents, but not necessarily a negative one.

The pastoral policy of the school, stressing the aims for the community, should be the centre of the school universe; the pastoral system should make clear the lines of care, command and communication within the system. What then is the role of the tutor in all of this?

The question of whether newly qualified teachers should have the responsibility of a tutor group is a matter of some debate. The stresses and strains of being a classroom teacher are exhausting enough for the teacher fresh from the relatively sedate life as a student – is having a tutor group not an unnecessary additional burden? My response would be that far from increasing pressure on new teachers, having your own tutor group can actually serve to reduce the strain.

New teachers face the same concerns and fears as new students in a new secondary school: What will it be like? Will I succeed? Will anyone like me? In the same way that a pastoral system exists to reduce such pressures and induct students into a shared set of values within a family, so too can it serve to induct the teacher. The tutor group can serve to create what has been referred to as 'a psychological and physical base' (Dean 1993, p. 21) If anyone were to doubt the need to form relationships and to create the essential pastoral element to education, then to view the way in which some classes can respond negatively to supply teaching would be proof enough.

As a new teacher you will inevitably be tested, throughout your first few weeks in particular, until you are 'accepted' into the school community by the students. For this reason the second year of teaching is often much easier. By having a tutor group the new teacher is able to forge pastoral, or 'human' links with her or his tutees, which can have a beneficial knock-on effect with other students with whom he or she comes into contact. Students talk to one another, and new teachers are a fascinating source of conversation in the first few weeks in a new school.

To be aware of the importance of your human responses to a tutor group can perhaps serve to heighten apprehension before a first post. This is not helped by the fact that the role of the tutor is one for which new teachers have historically felt drastically under-prepared. The Science teacher will have studied her or his subject for over three years now and should feel comfortable with her or his curriculum area and the requirements of the classroom teacher. What on earth is he or she supposed to do as a *tutor*?

Marland and Rogers have described the tutor as being the very heart of the school; the 'integrative centre for the school's efforts from attendance to welfare, study skills to behaviour' (Marland and Rogers 1997, p. 1) This is clearly a daunting task, but for those new teachers who may be in danger of feeling themselves to be a very small cog in a very large machine, it is again worth reminding oneself of the aims of education and the very real effect that the teacher, and particularly the tutor, can have in shaping a child's destiny: 'One of the most daunting but also encouraging aspects of responsibility for pastoral care is the research confirmation that success at school [in the broadest sense of the word] positively effects most aspects of later life' (p. 1).

Within the comprehensive system of equal entitlement to education it is the professional role of each teacher to ensure that children have equal access to the curriculum and their own personal and social development. In reality, however, the strongest responsibility rests upon the tutor, 'to ensure that students don't slip through the net' (Tubbs 1996, p. 68); to support and enable every student to achieve their potential and to gain the opportunities to which they are entitled. This fundamental right should be outlined in the school's pastoral care policy, but paper in files achieve nothing; it is the tutor's professional responsibility to turn paper theory into reality.

Pastoral care has been defined as containing four interrelated dimensions: welfare, curricular, administrative and disciplinary (Baumann, Bloomfield, Roughton 1997, p. 316). The tutor's 'roles' can be explained according to these four categories; however a tutor would be failing her or his students, and herself or himself, if the fundamental 'nurturing' role was not in place within the tutor group. Only within a caring and supportive environment can the personal and social development for which we all strive occur:

> If there were no tutors in a school there would be no 'home' for a pupil to go to when he or she needed it... At its best a home encourages self-esteem, develops judgement, creates a sense of coherence and provides security. (Marland and Rogers 1997, p. 1)

The tutor is the one fixed point of stability in the school, hopefully for the duration of a student's school life. It is worth bearing in mind that in many cases the tutor may be the *only* point of stability in many children's lives throughout a tumultuous period of personal and social development.

Pastoral care policy and systems require that all teachers are aiming for the same targets. Only if all teachers are aiming for the same culture can such an ambition be achieved. It is the responsibility, therefore, of each tutor to ensure that they are always acting in accord with the policies and practices of their school. To plough one's own separate furrow, aiming to achieve one's own personal aims, is not only unprofessional but also fundamentally selfish and misguided as it will inevitably undermine the whole school approach to child development.

The disciplinary role of the tutor can sometimes create a psychological dichotomy in that the good tutor will have built up a pastoral relationship with all his tutees and may be reluctant to endanger good relations. Indeed it is the tutor's professional responsibility to find value in all students; 'difficult' students need this stability and value perhaps more than any others in the school system. Whole-school disciplinary policies and practices must be adhered to however, if they are to be effective in creating the caring and safe environment within which learning can usefully occur. Reports of misbehaviour must be addressed with tutees, and to duck from such responsibility would undermine the respect a tutor has from her or his tutor group, including those students who may find themselves in trouble. The tutor does, however, have the benefit of being able to talk incidents through with tutees away from the environment within which that conflict occurred – 'at home' as it were. Teachers – and tutors in particular – are in the business of teaching behavioural skills. It is quite possible to follow up a disciplinary matter with a positive conclusion, if the pastoral aims of the school are working: 'It is particularly important to remember that students' misdemeanours offer opportunities for learning [for all]' (Dean 1993, p. 129).

The tutor group indeed affords genuine opportunities to establish group norms and an understanding of what behaviour is wrong and how such behaviour can be best corrected. It is important that whilst such a result might be achieved in the *presence* of the tutor group, it is essential that students are not humiliated in the process. A quiet discussion with a student can be discrete, but still send clear messages to the rest of the group, who will hopefully be engaged in other activities at the time. The conversation is private but noticed.

If tutors are to prevent students falling through the pastoral net, it is essential that the professional responsibilities in respect of what may seem the mundane matters of record keeping and monitoring of students' progress are understood. The twice daily register is a legal document for which tutors may be held to account. Registers need to be kept accurately and absences accounted for fully, in line with national legislation and the school's own policies. Absence letters should be kept for future reference and tutors need to be conscious of possible deceit from students with regard to such absences. To ignore possible truancy is to fail those students for whom the tutor has responsibility. Patterns of absence may also be noticed and if they are these should be brought to the attention of the tutor's pastoral line manager – the Head of Year or Head of House, in a secondary school, the head teacher in a primary school. Again, the opportunity to be seen to be chasing up suspicious absences in front of the tutor group sends clear signals about group norms and may dissuade some students from taking the risk of truanting. As with more serious crime, the major dissuading factor is not the severity of the sentence, but the likelihood of getting caught. The tutor also has the opportunity to show a caring side in such circumstances. Where the 'difficult' tutee has built up a strong and trusting pastoral relationship with the tutor – the one fixed point of stability, perhaps – the tutor's clear personal disappointment with wrong doing might have a more influential effect than an impersonal 'telling off'.

Monitoring of students is now developing in schools on a more formalised basis, as pastoral and curricular matters are brought closer together. Teachers need to be aware of the systems in place for monitoring student progression and to fully adhere to them. Again, the tutor, more fully in possession of knowledge of the whole student, is able to interpret and diagnose problems that may be occurring, or to praise where progress is being made.

Where developing difficulties can be diagnosed, the pastoral efforts of the tutor may enable intervention to pre-empt behavioural problems. Alternatively, where relationships with some teachers are problematic for the tutee, the tutor may be able to help resolve matters before there is a breakdown. Clearly there are potential problems for the tutor here, and new teachers need to be wary of their ignorance when it comes to the complicated and political nature of staff rooms; as with most other aspects of the job, if in doubt ask your Pastoral line manager for advice. It may help on occasions to simply allow the student to vocalise personality differences. It may indeed be a valuable lesson to learn that sometimes you need to simply keep your head down, understand that not all relationships can be perfect and get through the year; the tutor is not a magician after all, but he or she is capable of helping students to develop coping mechanisms.

A legal requirement of the tutor's professional role is to understand one's role with regard to potential child abuse.

> All teachers should be trained to identify signs of abuse in children. Any concerns *must* [my italics] be reported to the designated teacher or the head. A note of the teacher's concern should also be logged. (Marland and Rogers 1997, p. 74)

The tutor or teacher who sought to follow her or his own, independent, line with regard to such matters would be not only failing professionally, but also in breach of the law. With respect to confidentiality, it is clear from the Children Act (1989) that the welfare and protection of the child are overriding considerations, such that 'teachers can only guarantee confidentiality if in doing so there would be no serious risk to the pupil' (Elliott 1991, p. 164). Teachers and tutors should never promise confidentiality to students; to do so would put both the child at risk and the teacher in great risk of losing her or his job (see Chapter 3 for a discussion of child abuse and child protection).

The building of trusting relationships with tutees and students generally is a complex issue, upon which we do not have space to dwell here, but the importance of not putting oneself in a vulnerable situation cannot be stressed too highly. Union advice to teachers has made it clear that any one to one interviews with students should occur in a public environment, where the possibility for allegations against the teacher is negated. Leaving doors open – 'let me just get some fresh air in here' – or ensuring that teachers are never alone (in a room) with a student are essential, if regrettable, pieces of advice in these litigious times. You may find that your school's own policies now directly address such matters.

Bullying

The need to build a relationship of trust and confidence between tutor and tutee is a fundamental part of the anti-bullying policies that Elton himself recommended. If a pastoral policy's aim of creating a safe and caring environment is to mean anything, then the tackling of bullying must be a fundamental part of a school's approach.[1]

It is now generally accepted that bullying happens in all schools, regardless of the location or intake of that school. However, fundamental problems with the introduction and effective implementation of such policies appear to have been at least partly due to a cynicism on the part of teachers to recognise the extent of bullying in their schools. To deny the seriousness of the issue can only serve to cause further harm to the personal and social development of both the bully and the victim. In a survey by Glover and colleagues one Deputy Head is quoted as saying that, 'the whole thing is out of proportion, bullying is a buzz-word and becomes the excuse for any failure in relationships' (Glover, Cartwright, Gleeson 1998, p. 108). Glover and colleagues see such teacher-cynicism as mirrored in the comments that students make with regard to the effective application of such policies.

What then is the purpose of an anti-bullying policy?

> The rationale for having such a policy apart from satisfying increasing expectations that every school should have them, is usually threefold. A policy makes clear to everyone in the school community what the school is doing about bullying and why; it communicates clearly that bullying is not tolerated, and it can be used to monitor progress. (Glover, Cartwright, Gleeson 1998, p. 52)

Defining bullying is a major part of the problem in seeking acceptance of the policy by pupils and teachers. One school's policy document begins as follows:

> ***Bullying takes place in all schools***
>
> ***Bullying is the wilful, conscious desire to hurt or threaten or frighten someone else***
>
> ***Bullying can take many different forms***
>
> ***Bullying can be:***
>
> *Damage to property; graffiti; borrowing without permission; vandalism; silent pressure; ignoring; refusing to sit next to; group pressure; invading privacy; name-calling; ridicule; spreading rumours; passing notes; heckling; fighting; extortion; intimidation; physical violence; incitement.*
> (Baumann, Bloomfield, Roughton 1997, p. 127)

Clearly such a policy encompasses a very wide range of behaviours; however, it is essential that the creation of the definition should in itself be acceptable to teachers whose role it is to implement and address the very real problems in schools. If such a consensus is not formed at the very outset then such policies will have little real effect. Successful policies should reflect the shared aims of all in the community.

The professional teacher must, however, act in accordance with the finalised policy, whatever their personal reservations. The behaviour of many *teachers* might indeed be called into question with regard to such a policy. *All* members of the school community need to be acting in accordance with the philosophy, and bullying of students by teachers can only undermine the credibility of a school's intentions. Teachers who 'never have problems in my classroom' as was once boasted to me, are failing the school as a whole and students in particular if their only form of classroom control is terror. It is not difficult to instil fear into 12 year olds, but it is a challenge to create a respectful and human relationship within which true learning can, in its broadest sense, take place.

Where teacher scepticism as to the nature of the problem and the very policy remains, anti-bullying policies will not work. Regrettably Elliott's detailed research into the nature and effectiveness of such strategies reported a great deal of inconsistency in the way in which policies were implemented by teachers:

> The varied experience of those schools which have adopted anti-bullying policies indicate that the most significant factor in securing change is the encouragement given by *all* staff [my italics] to whole-school development. (Elliott 1991, p. 166)

If such policies are to have any real meaning in the classroom and wider school environment, it is essential that specific issues such as homophobia, racism and sexism are directly addressed in their own right and not simply subsumed into a general policy document. Specifically acknowledging and referring to these issues not only highlights the school's stance but also serves to eliminate any potential ambiguity, amongst students and teachers. Whilst schools have undoubtedly made great strides in addressing racism and sexism, the issue of homophobia has, regrettably, yet to receive the same prominence.

The continuation of bullying even in the most positive school environments is clearly grounds for concern, but perhaps most indicative of the failures of many existing systems to date has been the reluctance of the students themselves to respond to the anti-bullying structures that are in place. There is a clear cultural divide to be crossed when only 26 per cent of the students in one of the largest surveys felt that they would turn to their tutor if they became victims of bullying (Glover, Cartwright, Gleeson 1998, p. 108). The reluctance of children to respond must to a certain extent be a reflection of their perception that teachers would not take the matter seriously, perhaps a correct perception in light of comments outlined above.

The failure of teachers to have built up a strong and trusting relationship with tutees in their pastoral care has been revealed by the clear indication that students lacked confidence in the way in which teachers would handle incidents. Concern was expressed that teachers would betray the confidence of their students. Clearly this a particularly difficult bridge to overcome in light of the fact that teachers have not only a moral but a legal duty to ensure that children are not put at any risk. Where clear policies exist they must be applied; however, a better understanding of those policies by the students themselves might reduce this divide. A well formulated policy would, hopefully, be supported by students and contain a certain element of flexibility. Clearly a policy that dogmatically requires an unstoppable, inhuman, machine to creak into action in response to a child 'being ignored' by former friends is not one likely to succeed in its aims. Often students may simply need supporting at times of relationship breakdowns, and learning to cope with and deal with such matters is a skill which all students will require to lead emotionally secure lives during and after their school years. This is the very aim of Mosley's 'circle-time' initiatives: the empowering of students to cope independently with the situations and social problems that they will face beyond and after school life.

Fundamental to any successful pastoral policy is the building of a reliable and trusted pastoral relationship with the tutor. It is worth bearing in mind that despite the reluctance of students to approach teachers with regard to such problems, they have still been found to be second only to the student's 'best friend' when children are asked to whom they would turn if they were bullied (Glover, Cartwright, Gleeson 1998, p. 166).

All student teachers will have faced the horror and disbelief of friends and family when they mention that they wish to work in a modern, comprehensive, secondary school. This is largely a misconception of the anarchy that is perceived to exist in our contemporary learning establishments. It is a fear based upon adults' experiences of adolescents outside the school gates, on buses and on our streets in the evenings. It is based upon the perception that the decline in moral and behavioural standards – to which reference has already been made – must make our schools hellish places to work. It is a fear based upon the perception that our schools must mirror our society.

For the new idealistic teacher – and if you are not idealistic why are you going *into* teaching? – there are lessons that could be taught immediately to those sceptics. The relative order of our larger schools, containing over 1,000 adolescents in a small area, makes it clear that something *is* actually *working* here; a microcosm of society is in existence where order can come from potential chaos.

With the successful implementation of whole-school policies and practices our schools could become even more caring, and therefore more successful, places. Rather than schools reflecting the negative aspects of the world outside, perhaps the professional teacher, carrying out the school's policies and practices, could be serving to make the world outside a kinder and more successful place for the young adults we are working with. Maybe one day our communities could mirror the values of our schools.

Conclusion

In light of the clear recommendations of the Elton Report that 'the most effective schools seem to be those that have created a positive atmosphere based on a sense of community and shared values' (Elton 1989: 8), it is all the more disappointing that the predictions of some observers seem to have been proven correct when fearing that the report would be 'another unintended victim' of the colossal changes facing the state education system over the last ten years (Wheldall (ed.) 1992, p. 97)

Educationalists, including teachers themselves, have persistently voiced concerns that the most important aspect of the teacher's job – the pastoral aim of seeking to create a positive and caring environment – has increasingly been marginalised with the introduction of market forces and the National Curriculum.

The most fundamental aspect of any school's role in the comprehensive system is to find and recognise equal value in all of its students. Whole-school policies and pastoral aims have, however, all too often remained little more than paper documents, with little real relevance to the school experiences of teachers and students.

Equal opportunities within the comprehensive system can only be a serious possibility when all schools fully recognise the wide variety of backgrounds and social problems experienced by students. Only through a strong and meaningful pastoral system can this be achieved, yet the pressures and strains on schools have inevitably led to an erosion of this priority in the face of the very real fiscal pressures they face. The effective implementation of whole-school policies has not been prevented through any lack of willingness on the part of the school communities, but by the very harsh choices that many schools have been forced to make through the introduction of Local Management of Schools, league tables and the National Curriculum.

Whilst the aim of a pastoral and academic fusion is understood, the reality of the conflicting pressures facing schools is that the day to day emphasis has been increasingly on the academic; on material and quantifiable 'results'. The emphasis of government policy has been so firmly on the academic that the pastoral nature of the school – the recognised key to achievement – has been largely ignored. Pastoral matters are only newsworthy when schools are perceived to have reached breaking point, the media circus of The Ridings, in Halifax, being a prime example, when discipline was perceived to have become so bad that the school was closed for a short period and a new head teacher brought in to deal with this 'crisis-school'.

The academic demands of the National Curriculum immediately threatened the very intentions of the Elton Report, stressing so heavily the academic in the school system. Choices are inevitably made within the finite time and energy budgets of a school's staff:

> Make no mistake; the National Curriculum calls for sacrifices... More compulsory subjects mean more subject time and less time on those despised theories... When schools should have been taking on board the report's proposals they are, in fact, primarily engaged in coping with LMS and preparing to implement the National Curriculum. (Wheldall *et al.* 1992, p. 97)

The 'free-market' of the 1990s' education system appears in itself to abdicate responsibility for any pastoral care policy for the schools operating within it. Can we realistically expect schools on their own to concentrate on the building of children's self-esteem when such a system in itself generates 'sink' schools? Children attending such schools are often precisely those who most need to experience the reality of 'equal value', yet from the first day in their school those students are very well aware that their school is less 'valued' than an 'academically successful' school that is draining the soul and spirit from these contemporary secondary moderns.

Even within the most genuinely 'comprehensive' comprehensives, the focus on league tables has increasingly channelled schools' energies upon those borderline C/D students who could make all the difference when local newspaper editors draw up their headlines to be seen by next year's prospective parents. The very existence of league tables for five A-C grade GCSEs has, with a sweep of the pen, destroyed all of the hopes and aims that the GCSE system would provide an 'equal value' qualification that avoided the failures of the old system.

The GCSE results in 1998 provided perhaps an early indication that students are indeed 'slipping through the net' with a gap becoming all too apparent between the 'successes' and 'failures' of our academic system. Boys in particularly seem to be increasingly disaffected and underachieving, often seeking to compensate for their own personal low self-esteem through misbehaviour or the bullying of those apparently succeeding ahead of them.

> Some kids do well and they get praised in class but I have never been like that and I know that the other kids like me because I am good for a laugh. (Wheldall *et al.* 1992, p. 110)

In Glover, Cartwright and Gleeson's (1998) survey the work ethic was found to be particularly frowned upon by boys. Eight per cent of victims of bullying were reported as being singled out for 'working too hard'; 13% became targets because of 'being clever' (p. 110). In such circumstances both the bully and the victim were failing to benefit from any effective pastoral care or anti-bullying policy.

Behavioural problems are increasingly being brought into the mainstream classroom as the equal value notion of inclusive education sees special schools facing closure and fiscal pressures of their own. Without a clearly understood and effective pastoral care policy within mainstream schools, hopes of academic opportunities for all are simply unrealistic. Without time and money being invested into the development of mutually supportive environments, such policies cannot be seen as anything more than short-term cost-cutting.

The short-termism of government education policies has inevitably led to a desire to see tangible results that can be clearly put before the electorate as 'proof' of success before elections. Real progress for education can only be made by longer-term investment in the foundations of the education system: in building the self-esteem of *all* our children. Pastoral care policies and the building of a positive whole-school culture should be the *heart* of our education system, not a disposable add-on. Any attempt to improve the health of our schools that does not focus fundamentally on the heart will be ultimately doomed to failure. Pastoral care systems are the way we enable our children to become more human. They must be allowed to work.

Note

1. Kidscape have produced three personal safety programmes, which include lessons on dealing with bullying, for different age groups:
   Under-Fives programme (3–5 years and special needs children).

   Primary Kit (6–11 years).

   Teenscape (12–16 years).

Bibliography

Baumann, S., Bloomfield A., Roughton, L. (1997) *Becoming a Secondary School Teacher.* London: Hodder & Stoughton.
Dean, J. (1993) *Managing the Secondary School.* London: Routledge.
DfEE (1994) *Code of Practice on the Identification and Assessment of Special Educational Needs.* London: HMSO.
DfEE (1998) Circular 4/98 *Teaching: High Status, High Standards.* London: HMSO
Elliott, M. (1991) *A Practical Guide To Coping In Schools.* London: Longman.
Elliott, M. (1994) *Primary Child Protection Programme – Good Sense Defence.* London: Kidscape.
Elliott, M. (1995a) *Under 5's Programme.* London: Kidscape.
Elliott, M. (1995b) *Teenscape – A Personal Safety Programme for Teenagers.* London: Kidscape.
Elton, Lord (1989) *Discipline in Schools – The Report of the Committee of Enquiry chaired by Lord Elton* (The Elton Report). London: HMSO.
Glover, D., Cartwright, N., Gleeson, D. (1998) *Towards Bully-Free Schools – Interventions In Action.* Buckingham: Open University Press.
Golding, W. (1954) *The Lord of the Flies.* London: Faber & Faber.
HMI (1989) *Personal and Social Education from 5 to 16.* London: HMSO.
Kidscape (no specific date) Three personal safety programmes, which include lessons dealing with bullying: *Under-Fives and Special Needs programme*; *Primary kit*; *Teenscape.* London: Kidscape.
Lawrence, D. H. (1995) *The Rainbow.* Harmondsworth: Penguin.
Marland, M. (1974) *Pastoral Care.* London: Heinemann.
Marland, M. (1994) Review of McGuiness' *Teaching Pupils and Behaviour, Times Educational Supplement,* 28 January.
Marland, M. and Rogers, R. (1997) *The Art of the Tutor.* London: David Fulton Publishers.
MGM (1955) *The Blackboard Jungle* (film).
Mosley, J. (1993) *Turn Your School Round.* Wisbech: LDA.
Mosley, J. (1996) *Quality Circle Time in the Primary Classroom.* Wisbech: LDA.
Tubbs, N. (1996) *The New Teacher.* London: David Fulton Publishers.
Wheldall, K. (ed.). (1992) *Discipline in Schools – Psychological perspectives on the Elton Report.* London: Routledge.

Chapter 6

Liaising with parents, carers and agencies

Dee Sweeney

Introduction

This chapter begins with some general points about liaising with parents/carers and with agencies responsible for pupils'/students' welfare. It then outlines some of schools' statutory requirements with respect to such liaison.

Communication with parents/carers

In order to encourage the active involvement and participation of parents/carers in their child's or young person's education, there is a need for regular, clear and effective communication between schools and parents/carers. Communication can be written, as in prospectuses, reports or letters home. It can be verbal, such as telephone conversations and face to face meetings. It can take the form of consultation about policies within the school, which schools and parents/carers need to reach agreement on, or documents relating to home-school agreements (see later in chapter). Communication can be formal, as is the case with Parent Teacher Associations or Governing bodies. All teachers should be fully aware of their school's procedures for liaising with parents/carers. In particular, the following points should be borne in mind.

- Whenever a parent/carer approaches the school, the school should always be welcoming. The parent/carer should be aware of who they need to contact, whether it be for information or to discuss issues of mutual interest or concern. The parent/carer has a right to a prompt, constructive and helpful response. With respect to complaints, schools need to have clear procedural guidelines.
- Schools should be sensitive to the nature and structure of the pupil's/student's family/carers. They should know if the pupil/student lives with their birth parent(s) or with carers, or whether they are being looked after by the local authority or other agency. This will ensure that the correct form of address will be used: it would be inappropriate, for example, to send a letter beginning 'Dear Parents' if a child is not living with both parents.

- Schools need to be aware that the first language of the parents/carers may not be English. Thus, there may well be a need for an interpreter or translator.
- Schools need to ensure that there are appropriate services and facilities for parents/carers with disabilities.

Communication with agencies

Many agencies such as Health, Social Services, the Educational Psychology Service and the Police[1] have a statutory duty to work together with parents/carers and schools. Other organisations and agencies can enrich and complement the service provided for children and young people. They will include consultation agencies such as the LEA Advisory and Curriculum Departments, health promotion organisations, drug, solvent abuse and alcohol agencies, HIV/AIDs agencies, the Youth Service, as well as voluntary agencies, such as Include, and the National Children's Bureau. All of these agencies and organisations can provide advice and guidance, and can suggest appropriate strategies for a variety of school policies and procedures.

Circumstances will often necessitate the need for different agencies to work with the same child. For example, a pupil/student who has been excluded or has truanted *could* be under a Children's Service Plan, a Behaviour Support Plan, an Educational Development Plan, a Youth Justice Plan, a Drug Action Strategy. With such a multi-agency approach, there is a risk of duplication; thus it is essential that all agencies collaborate – if not one agency may end up taking the majority of the responsibilities – and that agency could be the school.

An understanding of the roles and parameters of the different agencies necessitates a proactive, constructive, collaborative approach. Teachers and schools need to identify local agencies, determine the appropriate person to deal with, and clarify the exact role agencies can play in a joint plan of action. Collaboration is the key element in providing services which meets the needs of children and young persons. We have an obligation to provide an effective inter-agency and partnership approach, so that children and young people receive the best service possible, in the context of mutual trust. This does not come automatically and has to be actively worked towards.

Government requirements and recommendations

Written communication

The Government's White Paper, *Building Excellent Schools Together*, emphasises the need for parents/carers to receive accurate information from schools:

> to be effective partners, parents need accurate information and regular feedback about what is happening in schools...No single document or information source can do this. What matters is that the information taken as a whole is user-friendly, and enables parents to make a balanced judgement of a school's achievement. (DfEE 1997, para. 2)

All schools must produce an annual prospectus. DfEE Circular 8/98 outlines the content of the secondary school prospectus and makes suggestions for optional additions. DfEE Circular 7/98 does the same for primary schools.

All teachers have a statutory responsibility to produce at regular intervals and at least once a year, clear, informative reports for the parents/carers on a pupil's/student's progress and attainment. This must include end-of-Key Stage results data.

OFSTED (1997), in their report *Secondary Schools 1993–97: Ethos, Behaviour and Pupil Support*, emphasised that teachers should 'report on weaknesses as well as strengths in pupils' progress and attainment'. It considers that the omission of reporting about the pupil's weaknesses, both in the pupil's progress and attainment and/or in the subject-specific targets which pupils need to address, is a major flaw in school report writing. Discussions are taking place between the Government, the DfEE and professionals about whether reports could include indications as to what parents/carers might be expected to do to help their child reach his or her full potential.

Home–school agreements

Home–school agreements set out the rights and responsibilities of the school, of teachers, of parents/carers and pupils/students and clarify what is expected of each. The details of the agreement are intended to match the requirements of the school, parents/carers and pupils/students. However, they would contain expectations about attendance, behaviour and discipline, homework, attainment, the standard of education and the ethos of the school.

They could include the rights of a free place at school and an education provided by professional staff, geared to the pupil's needs.

Homework

Government guidelines, which are available publicly (see Bibliography), recommends that schools should have a written policy on homework. The policy should provide guidance and information for pupils on the role of parents/carers and teachers (including how this role changes as the pupils get older), and arrangements for feedback from teachers and parents/carers. It should ensure that homework arrangements are manageable for everyone. It is the responsibility of the classroom teacher to ensure, on a day to day basis, that the demands of homework are manageable for pupils and parents/carers. OFSTED (1995) stated that 'many pupils and parents saw work done at home as a valuable and essential part of school work', while the Government White Paper *Excellence in Schools* talks of the 'vital role well organised homework could play in raising standards of achievement by pupils of all ages' (1997).

OFSTED (1997) commented that 'homework makes the greatest contribution to learning when:

- children and parents or carers are very clear about what they need to do;
- parents and carers are treated as partners in their children's learning;

- there is a regular programme so that everyone – teachers, children and parents or carers – know what to expect each week.

Teachers may, in some cases, need to provide suitable venues for homework outside the home, such as homework clubs. In some primary schools there are reading workshops for parents/carers which demonstrate the methods and techniques the school uses in the classroom.

Special educational needs (SEN)

Parents/carers with children having special educational needs often face exceptional pressures. To help them to cope, strong partnerships are required between parents/carers, schools, LEAs, Health, Social Services and other statutory and voluntary agencies. Only by having 'real' partnerships will children with special needs have opportunity to reach their full potential.

One of the fundamental problems regarding these children is that it is very difficult to define what special educational needs are. The law states that a child has special educational needs if he or she has:

- a *learning difficulty* (i.e. a significant greater difficulty in learning than the majority of children of the same age), or a *disability* which makes it difficult to use the educational facilities generally provided locally; and if that learning difficulty calls for
- special educational provision (i.e. provision additional to, or different from, that made generally for children of the same age in local schools). Whether or not a child has SEN will therefore depend both on the individual and on local circumstances (1998).

This implies that there may be inconsistencies between schools; one school may assess a child to have SEN and another school may not do so. This inconsistency may cause frustration for not only parents/carers but teachers as well. The *Code of Practice on the Identification and Assessment of Special Educational Needs* (DfE 1994) gives statutory guidance to schools, LEAs, Health Authorities and Social Services.

The Code of Practice outlines five Stages.

Stage 1 and *Stage 2* are school based and include drawing up an Individual Education Plan (IEP) which sets out targets for the child.

Stage 3 is also school based and involves the school accessing support from outside agencies, such as the Educational Psychology Service or LEA Learning Support Staff.

Stage 4 is a transitional stage, where the LEA considers the need for, and, if appropriate, arranges a multi-agency assessment of a child's special educational needs. During this stage, the school will continue providing support as in Stage 3.

Stage 5 is where the LEA considers the need for a Statement of Special Educational Needs and, if appropriate, draws up a statement and arranges, monitors and reviews provision for the child.

At all Stages parents/carers are fully consulted and kept informed. They need to be confident that schools will provide effective help for their child, especially at the first three Stages. This assurance could be strengthened by schools formulating a contract between themselves and parents/carers, which includes:

(a) a definition of the child's needs;
(b) the specific provision the school will provide to meet the child's needs;
(c) to clearly identify who will do what.
(DfE 1994).

For schools to effectively provide a suitable service they need to work closely with LEAs and access the educational psychologist and LEA Learning Support Staff. This could entail the outside agencies working with children within schools and helping teachers to improve their skills.

Parents/carers need to play a key part in their child's education. As Secretary of State for Education and Employment David Blunket clearly states:

> we want all parents of children with special educational needs to get effective support from the full range of local services and voluntary agencies, to have a real say in decisions about their child's education and to be empowered to contribute themselves to their child's development. Some parents need to be helped to gain access to these opportunities. (DfEE, 1998, Foreword)

Discipline, attendance and behaviour

Schools have a statutory duty to have a written discipline policy, and it is recommended that it has a whole-school approach. Parents/carers need to be fully aware of the discipline policy. Procedures should also include a system of rewards for good behaviour and should address the issues of bullying (see Chapter 5 for a discussion of bullying).

Parents/carers need to have a clear understanding of their legal responsibility to ensure their child attends school. The Education Welfare Service, in particular, plays a key role in working with parents/carers on their child's non-attendance.

DfEE Circular 1/98 gives guidance on the provision offered to pupils with behavioural difficulties and vulnerable pupils. Children who are considered to have behaviour difficulties include:

(a) those who have already demonstrated behavioural difficulties, such as
   - excluded pupils (both permanent and fixed term)
   - persistently disruptive pupils
   - pupils who have bullied others
   - violent or abusive pupils
   - pupils with statements of SEN for behavioural difficulties
   - pupils who have committed a criminal offence; or

(b) vulnerable pupils, such as those

- with emotional difficulties
- who have been bullied
- with mental health problems
- with significant trauma history, e.g. refugees
- on the Child Protection Register.

All LEAs have a statutory duty (Section 527A of the Education Act 1996) to formulate a Behaviour Support Plan. This plan should include details of current provision and proposed developments for whole-school strategies and support for individual pupils.

The plan should cover the following points:

- strategic planning of provision for pupils with behavioural difficulties, including arrangements for effective coordination between relevant local agencies;
- support to schools in improving the management of pupil behaviour with a view, amongst other things, of minimising unauthorised absence and exclusions;
- support for individual pupils with behavioural difficulties in mainstream schools;
- the type and nature of provision available outside mainstream schools for pupils with behavioural difficulties, including support for or re-integrating them into the mainstream where appropriate;
- arrangements for supporting pupils with behavioural difficulties;
- arrangements for such pupils who have special educational needs.

As schools have primary responsibility for managing the behaviour of their own pupils, identifying problems, conducting initial assessment of the needs of pupils and planning provision in the classroom, it is essential that schools are fully aware of the multi-agency support that they and parents/carers can access. The Behaviour Support Plan should provide them with this information.

DfEE Circular 1/98 outlines the expectations of schools:

- that the requirements of the SEN Code of Practice are followed for pupils with special educational needs arising from or causing behavioural difficulties;
- that the school liaises with others when necessary, including with the health service and parents and carers;
- that, in cooperation with parents, schools wherever possible endeavour to provide work for pupils to continue their studies while on fixed-term exclusions;
- that staff are offered adequate training in managing pupil behaviour; and school staff, and governors, follow statutory and locally agreed procedures and guidelines, for example, in handling absence and exclusions.

Schools and individual pupils may be able to access services, via the Behavioural Support Plan from behaviour support teams, the Educational Psychology Service, the Education Welfare Service, the Youth Service and other special counselling, advice and support services, such as Social Services, the Health services and Pupil Referral Units.

School support may involve:

- support and guidance in formulating a whole-school approach to discipline, attendance and behaviour;
- professional staff development in classroom and discipline management;
- classroom strategies for dealing with disruptive pupils, and the development of diagnostic skills for identifying and interpreting pupil behaviour.

Before approaching outside agencies, schools need to ensure that:

(a) the full needs of the pupil has been addressed, by having integrated discipline, pastoral and special needs policies;
(b) all staff are aware if a pupil is demonstrating behavioural difficulties and can identify the early indications;
(c) they have a range of approaches for dealing with difficult pupils, including support from the Special Educational Needs Coordinator (SENCO) and other members of staff;
(d) respective roles and responsibilities are clearly understood;
(e) they have a point of referral to external support which is clearly defined.

Circular 1/98 also stresses the importance of early identification and intervention, in order to prevent serious problems. It emphasises the importance of working with local outside agencies, such as health workers and social services who would be able to ascertain whether the behavioural difficulties stem from, for example, a medical condition or family problems.

It must be stressed that discipline, attendance and behaviour are often interlinked and hence provision must be made to reflect this.

In summary, a school needs to promote early identification and intervention for difficult pupils and identify and engage support from outside agencies.

Study support

Study support is defined, by the Government, as all learning activities outside normal lessons, whether they take place on school premises or not. The Government states that 'study support should be an integral part of young people's education, just as it is an integral part of the Government strategy for raising standards' (1997, para. 28)

Study support includes homework clubs, help with key skills, such as literacy and numeracy, study clubs, outdoor and sport activities, creative ventures and community services. It aims to benefit the school, parents/carers, pupils and community, by improving the pupils' academic standards and performance, by enhancing their self-esteem and confidence and by increasing motivation and creating a positive attitude towards learning.

Although study support is outside 'normal' school activity, schools and teachers still play a central role. Schools and teachers can liaise closely with a number of organisations. The Government's view is echoed by John MacBeath, a member of the DfEE Standards Task Force.

> good schools and good teaching are crucial to pupils' learning, their academic and other achievements at school and their prospects when they move on to further and higher education and to adult life. Yet effective teaching is not enough. Success for young people also relies on the homework and self-directed learning that they do out of school hours, and classroom learning flourishes when good teaching and self-directed learning meet. (MacBeath, 1998)

He goes on to say that

> for youngsters who have wide access to support from adults, books and equipment at home and the chance of interesting and stimulating outings in their spare time, study support is a bonus, an extra opportunity to enjoy learning. For others – especially those who are in danger of becoming disaffected or who have ceased to believe in themselves – study support can provide a more critical part of education. It can even make the difference between success or failure at school and in later life. (MacBeath 1998)

Family learning

Family learning can occur during the school day or as part of a study support scheme. The Government's White Paper *Excellence In Schools* (DfEE, 1997) states:

> parents are a child's first and enduring teachers. They play a crucial role in helping children learn. Family learning is a powerful tool for reaching some of the most disadvantaged in our society. It has the potential to reinforce the role of the family and change attitudes to education, helping build strong local communities and widening participation in learning.

The Government has in particular stressed what it sees as the key role parents/carers play in the improvement of literacy and numeracy. With respect to the former, it has emphasised the need for regular reading to and with parents/carers (1997). In a similar vein, the Numeracy Task Force recommended that schools should set number games and tasks which children can do at home which involves their parents/carers (OFSTED, 1997). Again, it is envisaged that parents/carers may require support in this.

Examples of *family learning* include:

- Setting up projects which involve bringing parents/carers into schools, e.g. parents/carers becoming classroom assistants who work with small groups of children (some parents have undertaken training to fulfil this role).
- A support mentoring scheme, i.e. responsible older people acting as 'foster' grandparents (Age Concern is liaising with the Government on this).
- Setting up projects to improve children's attitudes to education. This could include developing children's social skills (Home-Start volunteers work with families under stress in their own home).

The Government is expanding this initiative by using health visitors and school nurses to work with families who are reluctant to be involved or are unfamiliar with family learning.

Work experience

Work experience is seen as providing a forum for disaffected young people to become re-engaged and remotivated into education, school and community. It is seen as providing such young people with mentors and role models which they can 'relate' to, thereby providing a strategy for schools in dealing with difficult pupils (DfEE 1997, para 28)

Collaboration is the way forward in achieving a 'seamless' service for our children. However having a multi-agency approach produces its own problems. Increased liaison can produce an increase in paperwork; for example, consider the number of plans and strategies a child who has been excluded could be under: Children's Service Plan, Behaviour Support Plan, Education Development Plan, Youth Justice Plan, Drug Action Strategy.

Unless there is full cooperation, coordination, a complete understanding of roles and services provided, mutual trust and honesty, then there is a possibility that a child will 'fall' between all the strategies and plans. To guarantee that 'children do not fall' collaboration needs to be considered *not* as a luxury, or an *ad hoc* initiative, but as a core aspect of organisational management and thinking. Like adults, children and young people are not one-dimensional. They are complex, multifaceted beings whose lives cannot be compartmentalised into school, home, social and so on. All aspects of their lives interplay with each other. We must take into account all the circumstances and needs of the child or young person.

Note

1. There have been a number of revelations about racism in the police – for example, The Macpherson Report into the Lawrence Enquiry (with respect to the Metropolitan Police) and confirmations by David Wilmot, Chief Constable of Greater Manchester, and by Lloyd Clarke, the Deputy Chief Constable of West Yorkshire, that institutional racism exists in their respective police forces. In these circumstances, teachers and others involved with children and young people (and indeed those involved with the public in general) should be vigilant in their dealings with the police. Wilmot informed us that racism in Manchester ranged from verbal and physical abuse to stereotyping, and police attitudes in dealing with incidents on the street (*Guardian*, 14 October 1998).

Bibliography

DfE (1994) *Code of Practice on the Identification and Assessment of Special Educational Needs.* London: HMSO.

DfEE (1995) Circular 4/95 *Drug Prevention and Schools.* London: HMSO.

DfEE (1997) *Excellence in Schools.* London: HMSO.

DfEE (1998) Circular 1/98 *LEA Behaviour Support Plans.* London: HMSO.

DfEE (1998) Circular 7/98 *School Prospectuses in Primary Schools.* London: HMSO.

DfEE (1998) Circular 8/98 *School Prospectuses in Secondary Schools.* London: HMSO.

DfEE (1998) *Extending Opportunity.* London: HMSO.

DfEE (1998) *Excellence for all children: meeeting special educational needs.* London: HMSO

DfEE (1997) Consultation Document *Homework – Guidelines for Primary Schools.* HMSO.

DfEE (1998) Consultation Document *Homework – Guidelines for Secondary Schools.* London: HMSO.

Department of Health (1991) '*Working Together' under the Children Act 1989: A guide to arrangements for inter-agency co-operation for the protection of children from abuse.* London: HMSO.

OFSTED (1995) *Report: Homework is valued by pupils and parents.* London: OFSTED.

OFSTED (1997) *Standards and Quality in Education: Secondary Schools 1996/97.* London: OFSTED.

OFSTED (1997) *Standards and Quality in Education: Primary Schools 1996/97.* London: OFSTED.

OFSTED (1997) *Secondary Schools 1993–97: ethos, behaviour and pupil support.* London: OFSTED.

Social Exclusion Unit (1998) *Truancy and School Exclusion.* London: Social Exclusion Unit.

Chapter 7

The role and purpose of school governing bodies

Mark Drayton

'Be prepared – School Governors can be a funny lot'

The above quotation is a line from the 1997 film *Fever Pitch*, based on a novel by Nick Hornby, in which the head teacher tells the central character what to expect from his interview for the post of Head of Year.

The nature of governance is confirmed for us in the next scene, when we see the interview take place. One governor spends his time interrogating Colin Firth (who plays the football-mad teacher), as to his views on the potential outcome of Arsenal's season, while another governor spends time cross-examining Firth on his romance with another teacher and being, therefore, extremely personal.

Both portrayals, although amusing, paint a picture of incompetence, pettiness and unprofessionalism.

To this day, I believe that if 'the woman or man on the Clapham omnibus' was asked for their view on school governors they would hold something approximating this quaint amateur view of governing bodies. After all, who wants to be a school governor? Why be a school governor? Whether they are a 'funny lot', I will leave you to decide.

To fully appreciate the role and purpose of school governors today, I intend to outline governors' role in the curriculum, their legal duties and their role in the general running of the school. First, to appreciate where the position of school governor came from and how it has changed, I would like to put the office of governor in an historical context and look at some of the key legislation since the beginning of mass education in the nineteenth century.

The historical context of school governors

'The office of school governor can be traced back to the sixth century, but its modern origin is found in the work of early nineteenth century inspectors, appointed by the National and Foreign School Societies.' (East Sussex CC 1998, p. 3.) These were charitable societies concerned with educating the poor, and the role of inspectors was to ensure that grants from central government were used in the most effective and efficient way. The work of these societies highlighted the need for wide-scale reforms in education, and the practices of the inspectors strongly influenced the way in which subsequent legislation was framed. (For a fascinating historical account of the school governing bodies 597–1945, see DfEE 1997a, appendix B.)

Before the Education Act of 1870 three successive commissions were set up, initially to examine criticism of the style and quality of public schools (the Clarendon Commission 1861), then grammar schools and private schools (the Taunton Commission 1864), and last the needs of secondary schools in general (the Bryce Commission 1894). The relevance to the changing role for governors was that all three commissions laid emphasis on the role of local trustees or governors and the need to define their function in relation to those of head teacher; a continuing need today.

The following extract from the Report of the Clarendon Commission, attempts to define a governor's role, and at the same time outline the division between governors and the headteacher.

> Governors are the guardian and trustee of the permanent interest of the school. They should include people conversant with the world and with the requirements of active life. Governors should decide what should be taught and what importance should be given to each subject as well as appoint the headteacher and manage school property. The headteacher however should have charge of the division of classes, the school hours and school books, the measures necessary for maintaining discipline... (cited in East Sussex CC 1998, p. 3)

Of course this Commission was concerned largely with the nine public schools in existence at the time and at first glance the reference seems dated; for example there was no prescriptive national curriculum in 1861 so they, the Governors, chose it. But even today, governors have a large and increasing role in the curriculum and are legally bound to monitor it.

Education Act 1870

This was the year that marked the beginning of a country-wide system of elementary education, with secular provision filling the gaps. 'School boards were created in areas where such gaps existed and these were empowered to delegate many of their functions to bodies of local managers' (Sallis 1977, p. 117). The debate in Parliament on Forster's Education Act revolved largely around who should be responsible for managing schools. Some thought only the 'great and the good' should have this role. The National Education Union wanted schools to remain 'under the influence of the superior classes of society' (Hurt 1979, p. 79). After all, by 1895, over five million children had been brought into compulsory education and it was felt that 'whoever controlled the school could influence the education of the rising generation in a state that was moving slowly towards parliamentary democracy' (Hurt 1979, p. 78).

The state need not have feared that the school boards could in any way reflect society. By the late nineteenth century no more than around three per cent of board members were working-class men (Hurt 1979, p. 78). Something more was needed to make things more representative.

1902 Education Act

This abolished school boards and replaced them with Local Education Authorities (LEAs). These had total control over schooling. Therefore after 1902, governing/managing bodies were effectively squeezed out of any significant role, since they were wedged between the LEA and the day to day running of the school by the head teacher.

The governors did however appoint and dismiss head teachers, but by the 1920s:

> A paternalistic structure of school administration had been set up. It effectively excluded parents and teachers from any participation in the governance and management of schools. Neither did any school managing or governing body have to be accountable to anybody other than the local authority or central government. (Gann 1998, p. 14)

Butler's 1944 Education Act

This Act imposed a legal requirement for the establishment of governing bodies in schools: managers in primary schools, governors in secondary schools. Really nothing much had changed since the 1902 Act. However, educationally the 1944 Act was critical, setting a framework of primary, secondary and further education, but governors remained largely on the periphery. Only being required to meet three times a year, they had little to do with the monitoring and improving of education.

The Taylor Report 1977

This report was central to the changing role of governors in the postwar period and dared to suggest, much to the horror to the teaching profession, a structure and power balance similar to today. The report recommended governing bodies be made up of four equal parts:

(a) The LEA.
(b) The teaching and non-teaching staff.
(c) Parents.
(d) Individuals from the community.

These recommendations did not come out of thin air. Increased demands for governor involvement were boosted by a number of factors. First, local government reorganisation in 1974 brought about the demand for school-level decision-making, due to the increased size of the new LEAs. In addition, these new LEAs very often were made up of two old authorities, one of which wanted more governor say and one which did not. Something had to give. Second, the growth of comprehensive schools alerted the public to structures of education. Finally, and perhaps most importantly, there was pressure for change from the Parent Teacher Associations, the National Association of Governors and Managers, the Advisory Centre for Education and the Campaign for State Education.

They got what they wanted. Governors would be responsible for the aims of the school, would share in formulating the curriculum, in appointing staff and the head teacher and would have a four year term of office. However, the Labour Government vacillated; they endorsed the proposals but resisted the real changes in powers. By 1979, the Conservative Government were in power and since the Taylor recommendations fitted their right-wing agenda for education, by 1980 an Education Act had been implemented with the main recommendations of the Taylor Committee, including the obligatory election of parent governors.

The 1980s and 1990s

The Conservative Government passed a further Education Act in 1981 and in 1986 The Education (No. 2) Act followed the 'Better Schools' report (1985). The aim of this Act with respect to school governors was that it was supposed to revise the composition of governor bodies to give a more representative 'mix' and give governors a more clearly defined role. The Act emphasised the need to develop equal 'partnership' between governors, schools and the LEA.

The Education Reform Act 1988

This introduced the National Curriculum and National Standardisation of assessment and testing. Schools were given the option of becoming independent from the LEA through Grant Maintained Status (GMS). Very few took the option despite seductively large inducements from the Tory Government. For governors, our role was extended in terms of management, finance, staff appointments and general development of the school.

Education Acts 1992, 1993, 1996

Three further acts revised and extended previous legislation and introduced new responsibilities for governing bodies in relation to school inspections, curriculum issues and special needs education.

Education Act 1997

This Act was introduced just before the election with the agreement of all political parties. Some new concepts were introduced, such as baseline assessment at the beginning of Key Stage 1. This now meant that governors were legally responsible for most of what goes on in schools, especially after the implementation of the Local Management of Schools (LMS). They are also accountable to parents and the LEA. So are the governors really in charge?

The Roles, Responsibilities and Purpose of School Governors

Governing Bodies

Most governors' term of office is four years. The different types of governor are best described in *School Governors: The Guide to the Law* (DfEE 1997b). Legally the headteacher does not have to be a governor but has the right to attend all meetings. It may be difficult to imagine the governing body without the headteacher's input; he or she is the most important link the governors have with the school administration. It is extremely rare for a head teacher not to be a school governor. (For the composition of governing bodies, see Appendix 1, and for an example of a typical Governors' Meeting agenda, see Appendix 2.)

Stressing the importance of the role of the headteacher is not to underestimate the role of other teachers on the governing body and is certainly not the only way governors get to know the school. Most of us are bombarded with lists and guides to being a good governor from the LEA, OFSTED and the DfEE. While they are all useful, one wonders how many governors plough through this litany of information.

> The key characteristic of the effective governing body is the ability to understand and to implement the distinctive contribution it can make to the management of the school. (Gann 1998, p. 45)

To become effective therefore, governors need to get to know the school's needs, its special requirements and, most importantly, the needs of its staff and pupils/ students. This can be done in a number of ways and the 24,000 governing bodies (the total number of schools) are likely to have slightly different strategies. The following outlines how the school at which I am a governor tries to encourage that understanding by making the organic link between school and governing body.

My knowledge of how the school functions comes from school visits and these take many forms. They can be 'rota visits' whereby we agree to visit the school on specific dates and these visits take place at least once a term. These are coupled with other visits depending on which sub-committee, as a governor, one may be on. At my school there are sub-committees dealing with Buildings, Curriculum, Finance, Staffing and Staff Salaries. So if for example one were a serving governor on the Curriculum Sub-Committee, one would make regular visits to see how studies were progressing in action rather than simply relying on Standard Attainment Targets (SATs) results.

Perhaps the most important practical link at my school for me is my area of subject responsibility. This is early years education, and it is my job to keep abreast of developments and monitor progress. The strength of this strategy is that one becomes specialised in the area of responsibility (at least that is the theory) and one gets to know the teachers involved. One is encouraged to provide reports to the governing body. Gradually over the four years, as one's area of responsibility changes, one's effectiveness increases. Of course one cannot just enter the school unannounced, and some schools have policies providing clear guidelines on procedures and conduct during visits.

The Governing Body should work as a team. It is not therefore, expected that a single governor can see every aspect of school life in two or three visits a year. In addition, governors are not able to make numerous visits, given the time constraints on staff. The load is therefore shared with different governors specialising in the different areas.

The strategic view – a governor's role

The strategic role is considered increasingly important for school governors. Through strategic planning the governing body must help set up and keep under review the overall framework within which the head teacher and staff should run the school. The governors should focus on key issues; for example, promoting effective teaching and learning whilst trying to raise standards and expectations.

As stated by the DfEE in *Governing Bodies and Effective Schools*:

> The governing body has important powers and duties but limited time and resources. So it should focus on where it can add most value – that is, in helping to decide the school's strategy for improvement so that its pupils learn most effectively and achieve the highest standards. (DfEE 1995, p. 2)

To ensure accountability – a governor's role

Governing bodies have the responsibility of ensuring good quality education. Through the governors' meetings, visits and head teacher's reports etc., they should ascertain the school's progress. It is not the role of governors to simply rubber stamp the decisions of a head teacher.

> The governing body has a right to discuss, question and refine proposals while always respecting the professional roles of the head teacher and other staff and their responsibilities for the management of the school. In its turn the governing body answers for its actions, above all to the parents and the wider community for the school's overall performance. (DfEE 1995, p. 2)

Summary of responsibilities of the school Governing Body

The role governors play in the planning of a school strategy whilst making sure of accountability and being a 'critical friend' (see below) leads on to the specific tasks outlined under the law. (DfEE 1997b).

Legislation over the last ten years has increased the responsibilities and duties of governors. They now have to:

(a) Help draw up (with the head teacher and staff) the School Development Plan.
(b) Decide how to spend the school's budget.
(c) Select a head teacher.
(d) Appoint, promote, support and discipline staff.
(e) Act as a link between the school and the local community.
(f) Draw up an Action Plan after an inspection and monitor how the plan is put into practice.
(g) Make sure that the National Curriculum and religious education are taught.
(h) Decide the conduct of the school – in broad terms how the school is run.

Other issues spring from each of these areas. Under the 'Conduct of the School', other areas to be considered by governors are discipline (a policy has to be drawn up), attendance, truancy and exclusions.

The governor's role in the curriculum

With the National Curriculum being so prescriptive when becoming a governor, I had not envisaged governors having such a potentially huge role to play in this area. Under the 1988 Education Act, governors and the head teacher are supposed to secure a curriculum that is broadly based and:

(i) Promotes the spiritual, moral, cultural, mental and physical development of pupils at the school and of society.
(ii) Prepares such pupils for the opportunities, responsibilities and experiences of adult life.
(East Susssex CC 1998, p. 1)

The National Curriculum is compulsory for all children of school age and governors must make sure this is delivered. However, we can modify the LEA's policy statement to fit the needs of the individual school. Thus the school curriculum can be supplemented by other activities. If any modifications are made, the governors must consult the head teacher and the LEA, and have regard to any representation made by members of the community or bodies such as the local police, the church. The governing body then issues its own statement on the curriculum which includes the policy on collective worship, religious education, sex education and special needs education.

The governor's role in school inspections

The OFSTED inspection system was set up in secondary schools in 1993 and in primary and special schools in 1994. As governors we are responsible for agreeing with OFSTED the specifications for the inspection.

Governors also distribute the inspection summary to parents and ensure that parents can meet with the inspectors. We also ensure the report is published widely through the media and local libraries and we discuss the findings with inspectors and staff. Finally an Action Plan is agreed to address the findings of the OFSTED report and parents are informed of any progress made in the school's annual report.

Recent developments

The last two years have been a busy time for governors who have had to respond to further Government requirements. Following a White Paper in the Summer of 1997 called *Excellence in Schools* the School Standards and Framework Act has been produced and its provisions on governing bodies will be implemented in September 1999. Once again, it proposes clearer roles for schools, governors and LEAs in order to 'raise standards' and encourage devolved decision-making with the aim of directing more resources to schools. However, will these fine words amount to anything concrete?

In addition, more is required of governors with respect to the curriculum in the form of a baseline assessment of new pupils on entry at Key Stage 1. This was implemented in full in my area in September 1998. Governors find themselves in the situation of setting targets for an unknown intake of pupils, who are barely out of their babyhood.

As governors, we are also trying to gauge the effects of the National Literacy Scheme. This project, which features a daily literacy hour, was piloted in 1997 and extended to all primary schools in September 1998. New Labour's target is that, 'By 2002, 80 per cent of all eleven year olds will reach the standard expected for their age in English' (*Education Guardian*, 22 September 1998, p. 2). Only 55 per cent of 11-year-olds in my area attained this target in 1997. The literacy hour may well be a good idea but how far it will go to meet the 80 per cent target remains to be seen.

The actual role of governing bodies

Owing to the increasing demands on governing bodies and the growing research and observational studies being done, the focus is on the 'actual' role played by governing bodies.

Ian Jamieson, of the University of Bath, has divided governing bodies into three broad types. Although hard to quantify he suggests that roughly 80 per cent of governing bodies are no more than 'supporters' clubs'. He claims that governing bodies that fit this model do not do much more than 'cheer the school from the terraces', and approve the actions of the head teacher. (Jamieson, cited in Gann 1998, p. 44). If Jamieson is right, this means that approximately 19,000 schools have delegated effective control to the head teacher (Jamieson says largely by default rather than design). This means that when problems arise there is no effective body to deal with them and the school becomes the domain of the education profession rather than the communities they serve.

Jamieson describes the second type of governing body as the 'adversarial model'. This applies to some five per cent of schools. In these schools a system whereby the governors govern and the headteacher manages has not been found. There is conflict between the headteacher and governors and the head may see the governors as unrepresentative, aloof, interfering or prone to division. In these cases it is clear what the problems will be and it is these schools which the tabloid press enjoys focusing on.

The final category is the governing body that has achieved the status of a 'critical friend'. This, Jamieson says, accounts for about 15 per cent of governing bodies (Jamieson, cited in Gann 1998, p. 45). The role of the governor as a critical friend is increasingly being advocated by the DfEE, LEAs, and OFSTED in their literature; this may well be desirable bearing in mind the Bath study showing 80 per cent of school governing bodies being 'supporters' clubs'. Almost anything is better than that. The 'critical friend' role is easy for governors to understand. Since the governing body provides the head teacher and the staff with support, advice and information, it needs to be critical in the sense of its responsibility for monitoring and evaluating the school's effectiveness, and by asking challenging questions (e.g. 'Are vertical bands the best way of organising classes?'). The governors have to press for improvements in the school and be a 'friend' too as we exist to promote the interests of the school and its pupils.

This is one role my local LEA is encouraging. It seems to be a proactive phase to encourage governors to take a position on their roles in the school. The logic is probably founded on the basis that it is better to be a 'critical friend' than end up in the supporters' club role. OFSTED has been encouraging the critical friend role as a way of 'maintaining and improving the quality of education and standards of achievement' (OFSTED 1995, p. 67).

If these standards are not met, the Chief Inspector of Schools, Chris Woodhead, leaves us in no doubt who is responsible for a failing school:

> In a small but worrying proportion of schools, governors have been unprepared to deal with serious weaknesses, particularly those where the leadership shown by the head teacher or teaching competence of a member of staff is poor. (OFSTED 1996, p. 47)

The trouble with this viewpoint is that few governors enjoy disciplining or firing teaching staff. As governors we generally want only to do positive things for our schools. The problem with the Chief Inspector's ultimately right-wing 'survival of the fittest' logic is that it is based on the myth that there are a large minority of 'poor teachers'. Whatever the number, Woodhead fails to see that it is the system that is cracking at the seams and causing demands on teachers which are reaching intolerable proportions.

This kind of mentality is the very thing that is driving teachers out of the profession, whilst teacher education courses are undersubscribed. A confrontational approach is not what is meant by 'critical friend'.

Conclusion

This chapter began by addressing the developing historical role of governors and went on to examine the current roles and purposes of school governors and governing bodies. In so doing, I raised some general concerns. This section of the chapter will try to 'plug the gaps' and raise issues of concern, to me, about the role of governors. Are school governors able to deliver effectively on behalf of the school? If not, whose fault is it? How accountable are they? Just who are the school governors anyway?

Insularity

There is a strong, but understandable, tendency to be insular in one's approach as a governor. Governors consider only the school of which they are a governor. But this insularity leads to a lack of overall political understanding; for example it is unlikely that governors have a broad overview of the impact on education and teachers in general of Education Action Zones (EAZs), the so called 'superteachers' or sponsorship in schools.

If their school is selected as being part of an EAZ, governors are far more likely to welcome it on the basis of more money for their school and therefore the ability to balance the budget. They are less likely to entertain the potential damage which EAZs can inflict on the education system as a whole. Some commentators see them as the beginning of the privatisation of the education system. As Richard Hatcher has put it:

> Education Action Zones are intended to raise standards in 'socially disadvantaged' areas with what are regarded as underperforming schools.... Launching a well-funded, democratically-controlled, progressive and equitable initiative to effectively meet educational needs in poor working class areas is exactly what a Labour government should be doing. But New Labour's Educational Action Zones will be none of these things. Not only will they do little to solve the real problems of working class education, they are a Trojan horse for a new model for the entire school system which goes further down the Tory road than the Tories themselves dared. (Hatcher 1998, p. 4; see also Cole 1999)

Will school governors see the problem EAZs pose? Will they even raise any doubts? The answer is 'probably not', because it is seen as 'political'. Here we run into another problem. A recent study (Radnor and Ball 1996, p. 40) reported that head teachers significantly preferred governors to be non-political and portrayed governing bodies as non-political. Very often LEA governors are seen as political nominees who 'let political polemic get in the way of looking at our particular school and the children in it' (Radnor and Ball 1996, p. 40). Party politics at governor level was not appreciated. This is hardly surprising since, while their real agenda may have been to inject party politics into education, the last Tory government tried its best through social policy to *appear* to depoliticise service delivery and to make education *seem* neutral and value free.

The result is that school governors' accountability becomes narrowly defined in terms of efficiency and effectiveness. 'Attention is diverted away from the contents and processes of education toward its outputs and costs' (Radnor and Ball 1996, p. 41). The acceptance of a depoliticised public service shows up an operational weakness of the 'new voices in school government' and may simply swell the ranks of a consensual educational lobby.

Accountability

LEAs are responsible for all parent and governor elections. All parents can stand for election. Voting is by secret ballot. LEA governors are appointed through democratically appointed committees. Governors are answerable to the parents and the wider local community and there are LEA procedures to facilitate this. This all sounds fine. But words like democracy and accountability are bandied about so frequently, as if they are some new buzz-words, and they end up being used so widely, vaguely and incoherently that they become almost meaningless.

But governors *are* elected and they *are* answerable to parents and various committees, but not subject to instant recall. As Radnor and Ball's findings show:

> Governing bodies are now, in most schools, a major focus of influence, guidance and support. However, despite the rhetoric of legitimation offered by head teachers, their representativeness and accountability are partial, unclear and very uneven. (Radnor and Ball 1996, p. 65)

They go on to acknowledge the current powerful role school governors occupy, but claim they have an ambiguous position in the educational politics of the UK.

> Internal relationships between governors and head teachers are made to work most of the time in most schools. When they don't work major difficulties typically ensue. External relationships between governors and parents and the local community are also beset by vagary. The more general role of governors in mediating between the school and parents is markedly under-developed. (p. 65)

Recruiting school governors

Despite these extra burdens there is little evidence of a shortage of people willing to stand as governors. Of course there are regional variations and some London boroughs experience difficulties in getting a full complement of governors, but in 1991 it was found that:

> Only ten per cent of schools had fewer candidates than places for parent governors and only 1.2 per cent were short of teacher governors. Nor does there seem to be evidence of mass resignations of governors as the new responsibilities begin to be understood. It would seem that the new governing bodies contain significant numbers of committed and probably highly articulate people – the days of the governing body being packed by the local great and good are, in most places, over. (Beckett, Bell, Rhodes 1991, p. 14)

Through discussion with school governors in my area, and council officials, it seems that some areas are increasingly experiencing difficulties, as the increased responsibility of the school governor begins to register more widely amongst parents and the local community generally. Certainly my head teacher was pleased to have me as an LEA governor (if for no other reason than to have a full complement) and we still have problems co-opting governors from the local community and the business community as is required.

Where do governors come from?

The Conclusion to this book deals with issues raised in other chapters concerning class, 'race', gender, disability and sexuality, as well as issues related to equality and equal opportunities. Here, I briefly focus on who does make up the ranks of school governing bodies.

In April 1989 a report was commissioned by the DES to survey the new governing bodies as constituted under the 1986 Education Act, and establish whether they were being over-staffed by teachers standing as parent governors, co-opted governors or LEA appointees. The report laid these fears to rest. However it did find that governing bodies were predominantly white, male and middle class.

> Added together, the business, professional, retail and technical occupations and engineers accounted for 41.5 per cent of occupations reported, while a depressingly low 3.1 per cent were manual workers. The vast majority of governors were from the United Kingdom ethnic groups [sic] and in all categories the number of black or Asian governors was under three per cent – well under in most cases. There were significantly more male governors (57.1 per cent) than female (41 per cent), although in two categories – parent and teacher governors in primary schools – women were in the majority. (Beckett, Bell, Rhodes 1991, p. 14)

Having gone on training courses, talked to other school governors in my area, and knowing my own governing body, it is clear that this representational bias has not been addressed.

Research in the early 1990s sought to establish whether any changes in this situation had occurred since the 1988 Education Reform Act. There was little noticeable difference: schools still reported a predominantly professional/ middle class background for their governors.

> Of the eight reports, concerning primary schools, only one, relating to an inner city school in Tower Hamlets, reported a predominance of working class governors. As to the remainder, one from a working class area of Cornwall reported that middle class professionals constituted fifty per cent of members, but the remaining six reports suggest that the majority of governors were middle class. (Golby and Appleby 1991, p. 6)

Research by Gann (1998) has identified that among the minority ethnic communities, representation comes from the Asian rather than the African-

Carribean communities, while Deem and Brehony's (1995) survey found that only 31 per cent of governors were women.

There appears to be no concrete solution to the class, gender and ethnicity breakdown in school governance, without fundamental changes in the social system. The breakdown of who the school governors are, at least makes one aware that a lot is needed culturally, socially and politically before imbalances can be redressed. Measures such as time off with pay would go some way to widening participation, and crèche facilities and care over the timing of meetings would help. However, these are ultimately only accommodations and do not offer a real prospect of concrete change.

Let teachers teach and governors govern

As lay people, governors have various skills and experience to offer schools. Few have professional educational knowledge and yet as governors are asked to set targets, ratify discipline procedures, ensure the National Curriculum is delivered and so on. Some of these responsibilites are very specific and require detailed knowledge of education and child development. What do non-teacher governors know of such matters? All the training courses in the world will not make up for the professional knowledge of teachers and head teachers. Given this situation, it would be strange if governors were not to follow the advice of the head teachers, teachers and non-teaching staff who know the school's needs and capabilities.

Let the teachers teach and the governors govern. Governors will try to make sure schools have the resources they require to meet the needs of pupils/students, teachers and non-teaching staff. It should be people from the local community who become school governors, people who are *representative* of that community. Far better that powers be vested with them, than with so-called experts, or yet another quango. As Gann puts it:

> Whether we like it or not, we live in interesting times. Whether this will turn out to be the traditional Chinese curse, or a blessing for education, remains to be seen. (Gann 1998, p. 171)

I would put it a bit stronger than that. The teaching profession, unions, LEAs and governors can only do so much to deliver the kind of education our children deserve. But cracks are appearing. In the end, we are waiting for the New Labour Government to deliver its promises.

Bibliography

Bacon, W. (1978) *Public Accountability and the Schooling System.* London: Harper & Row.

Beckett, C., Bell, L. and Rhodes, C. (1991) *Working with Governors in Schools.* Buckingham: Open University Press.

Cole, M. (1998) 'Globalisation, Modernisation and Competitiveness. A Critique of the New Labour Project in Education'. *International Studies in the Sociology of Education* **8**(3) 315–332.

Deem, R. and Brehony, K. (1995) *Active Citizenship and the Governing of Schools*. Buckingham: Open University Press.
DfEE (1995) *Governing Bodies and Effective Schools*. London: HMSO.
DfEE (1996) *Guidance on Good Governance*. London: HMSO.
DfEE (1997a) *Taylor Committee Report*. London: HMSO.
DfEE (1997b) *School Governors: A Guide to the Law*. London: DfEE.
DfEE (1997c) *Excellence in Schools*. London: HMSO.
DfEE (1998) *Setting Targets for Pupil Achievement: Guidance for Governors*. London: DfEE.
East Sussex County Council (1998) *East Sussex Governor Support Programme*. Lewes: ESCC.
Gann, N. (1998) *Improving School Governance*. Lewes: Falmer Press.
Golby, M. and Appleby, R. (eds) (1992) *In Good Faith: School Governors Today*. Tiverton: Fairway Publications.
Hatcher, R. (1998) 'What's Wrong with Education Action Zones?'. *Socialist Teacher* **65**, Spring, 4–5.
Hurt, J. S. (1979) *Elementary Schooling and the Working Class 1860–1918*. London: Hart-Davis.
Kogan, Johnson, Packwood and Whitaker, (1984) *School Governing Bodies*. London: Heinemann.
Mahoney, T. (1988) *Governing Schools: Powers, Issues and Practice*. London: Macmillan.
OFSTED (1995)
OFSTED (1996)
Radnor, H. and Ball, S. (1996) *Local Education Authorities: Accountability and Control*. Stoke-on-Trent: Trentham Books.
Sallis, J. (1977) *School Managers and Governors: Taylor and After*. London: Ward Lock Educational
Wragg, E. C. and Partington, J. A. (1989) *A Handbook for School Governors*. London: Routledge.

Number of pupils registered	Up to 99	100–299	300–599	600 +*
Parent governors	2	3	4	5
Teacher governors	1	1	2	2
LEA governors	2	3	4	5
Co-opted governors	3	4	5	6
Ex-officio governors	1	1	1	1
Total governors	9	12	16	19

Appendix 1: The composition of governing bodies

* Schools with 600 or more pupils can either have the same as schools with 300–599 or the breakdown as shown in the table.

Source: School Governors: A Guide to the Law, DfEE 1997, p. 3.

Appendix 2: Typical Governors Meeting Agenda

Apologies
Welcome new governors
Election of Sub-Committees and Subject Coordinators
Minutes of the meeting 31 May
Matters arising
Correspondence
Headteacher's Report
SATs
OFSTED
Buildings
Curriculum
Development Plan.
Reports from the Sub-Committees: Staff Salaries and Finance
Governor Training
Date of: Next Governors' meeting
Finance committee
OFSTED Meeting with Parents
Governors' Feedback from OFSTED

Conclusion: where do we go from here?

Mike Cole

The contributors to this book are united by a belief in the importance of equality and equal opportunity for all.[1] Token recognition of the latter, if not the former, is acknowledged by the Government by its requirement in Circular 4/98, Annex A, Section D 'Other Professional Requirements' (hereafter referred to as A(D)) for all student teachers to 'have a working knowledge and understanding of... [their] legal liabilities and responsibilities relating to the Race Relations Act 1976 [and] the Sex Discrimination Act 1975' (DfEE 1998, p. 16).

Equality and equality of opportunity issues, I believe, should command a much higher profile. The aims of this Conclusion, then, are two-fold: first, to make some observations on legislation on equal opportunities; second, to make some suggestions as to what needs amending in the A(D) non school-based requirements, and to consider A(D)'s omissions. If the suggestions about changes in, and additions to, equal opportunity legislation do not have an immediate impact on Government policy (although I believe that in the longer term, changes and additions will occur), I believe there are good reasons for the TTA and the DfEE to incorporate the suggested amendments and omissions to A(D) in Circular 4/98's replacement.

Equal opportunities legislation

Given the continuing preponderance of racism, sexism, homophobia and discrimination directed at people with disabilities both in British society at large and within the education system (e.g. Waller, Cole and Hill 1999, Blair and Cole 1999, Kelly 1999, Martin 1999, Ellis and Forrest 1999, Forrest 1999, Rieser 1999a, b), there is a clear need for legislation dealing with these issues. Existing legislation on Race Relations and Sex Discrimination needs to be strengthened, in order to make it much more effective in combating racism and sexism, both in society at large and in schools. As far as the existing Disability legislation is concerned, the Disability Act 1995 has a number of weaknesses and changes and additions would make it more effective (Rieser 1999a; see also Chapter 2 of this volume).

A glaring omission in British equal opportunities legislation is a Sexuality Discrimination Act. Indeed, with respect to schools, legislation exists which actually promotes homophobia. Section 28 of the Local Government Act 1989 prohibits local education authorities 'intentionally promoting homosexuality', or promoting 'the teaching in any maintained school of the acceptability of homosexuality as a preferred family relationship'. The repeal of this legislation is long overdue and needs to be accompanied by legislation which makes it unlawful to discriminate on grounds of sexuality.

Further professional requirements

I have four major and interrelated suggestions to make about the improvement of A(D). First, with respect to A(D) a(ii) (see Figure 1, p. vi), while 'a working knowledge and understanding of' the various pieces of legislation is self-evidently important and worthwhile, there is an obvious need to include knowledge and understanding of the aforementioned Disability Discrimination Act of 1995 (this is recognised and addressed by Jeff Nixon in Chapter 2 of this volume).

Second, when (and I say 'when' because it is surely only a matter of time) legislation dealing with discrimination on grounds of sexuality is on the statute book, this should also be part of the professional requirements of A(D) a(ii).

My third suggestion concerns A(D)f. Where the need is specified to 'understand... professional responsibilities in relation to school policies', there should be a *specific reference* added here to equal opportunity policies. It is important that policies should encompass social class and sexuality as well as the more common policies on gender, 'race', disability and special needs.

My fourth suggestion is that a final requirement be added to A(D): since the last current requirement is h, let us call it i. Requirement i should be that all those to be awarded QTS (*in addition* to understanding professional responsibilities in relation to *equal opportunities policies in schools*) have knowledge and understanding of equality issues in general. Issues should include social class, 'race', gender, disability and special needs and sexuality. Such issues need attention in their own right and in relation to education, and they need to be considered both conceptually and empirically (e.g. Hill and Cole (eds) 1999a) and to be addressed both historically and in a contemporary context (e.g. Cole (ed.), 1999). Finally, equality issues need to be considered with respect to the individual subjects of the National Curriculum of both the primary and the secondary school (Cole *et al.* (eds) 1997, Hill and Cole (eds) 1999b).

As the TTA has taken more and more control of the teacher education curriculum, equality issues have been marginalised or neglected. It is high time to resurrect them. In a manifestly unequal society (e.g. Hutton 1995; Hill and Cole (eds) 1999b), which manifests itself in schools as much as everywhere else (Cole *et al.* (eds) 1997), it is meaningless to talk about preparing professional teachers to cater for the needs of *all* children and young people unless these issues are seriously addressed.

Note

1. A distinction needs to be made between equal opportunities on the one hand, and equality on the other. Equal opportunities policies, in schools and elsewhere, seek to enhance social mobility within structures which are essentially unequal. In other

words, they seek a meritocracy, where people rise (or fall) on merit, but to grossly unequal levels or strata in society – unequal in terms of income, wealth, life-style, life-chances and power. Egalitarian policies, policies to promote equality, on the other hand, seek to go further. First, egalitarians attempt to develop a systematic critique of structural inequalities, both in society at large and at the level of the individual school. Second, egalitarians are committed to a transformed economy, and a more socially just society, where wealth and ownership is shared far more equally, and where citizens (whether young citizens or teachers in schools, economic citizens in the workplace or political citizens in the polity) exercise democratic controls over their lives and over the structures of the societies of which they are part and to which they contribute. While equal opportunity policies in schools and elsewhere are clearly essential, egalitarians believe that they need to be advocated within a framework of a longer-term commitment to equality. Where they are not, the false assumption has been made that there is a 'level playing field', on which we all compete as equals. Plainly there is not. (Cole and Hill 1999)

Bibliography

Blair, M. and Cole, M. (1999) 'Racism and education: the imperial legacy', in Cole, M. (ed.) *Human Rights, Education and Equality.* London: Falmer Press.

Cole, M. (ed.) (1999) *Human Rights, Education and Equality.* London: Falmer Press.

Cole, M., Hill, D., Shan, S. (1997) 'Preface: A Society Divided', in Cole, M., Hill, D. and Shan, S. (eds) *Promoting Equality in Primary Schools.* London: Cassell.

Cole, M. and Hill, D. (1999) 'Introduction', in Hill, D. and Cole, M. (eds) *Promoting Equality in Secondary Schools.* London: Cassell.

Cole, M., Hill, D., Shan, S. (eds) (1997) *Promoting Equality in Primary Schools.* London: Cassell.

DfEE (1998) Circular 4/98 *Teaching: High Status, High Standards.* London: DfEE.

Ellis, V. and Forrest, S. (1999) 'One of them or one of us: sexuality, identity and equality', in Cole, M. (ed.) *Human Rights, Education and Equality.* London: Falmer Press.

Forrest, S. (1999) 'Difficult loves: learning about sexuality and homophobia in schools', in Cole, M. (ed.) *Human Rights, Education and Equality.* London: Falmer Press.

Hill, D. and Cole. M. (eds) (1999a) *Equality and Schooling: Conceptual and Empirical Issues.* Unpublished.

Hill, D. and Cole. M. (eds) (1999b) *Promoting Equality in Secondary Schools.* London: Cassell.

Home Office (1989) Local Government Act, Section 28. London: HMSO.

Hutton, W. (1995) *The State We're In.* London: Jonathan Cape.

Kelly, J. (1999) 'Gender and Equality one hand tied behind us', in Cole, M. (ed.) *Human Rights, Education and Equality.* London: Falmer Press.

Martin, J. (1999) 'Barbarians are at the gates: gender and education' in Cole, M. (ed.) (1999) *Human Rights, Education and Equality.* London: Falmer Press.

Rieser R. (1999a) 'Disability discrimination, the final frontier: disablement, history and liberation', in Cole, M. (ed.) *Human Rights, Education and Equality.* London: Falmer Press.

Rieser R. (1999b) 'Special educational needs or inclusive education: the challenge of disability discrimination in schooling', in Cole, M. (ed.) *Human Rights, Education and Equality.* London: Falmer Press.

Waller, T., Cole, M., Hill, D. (1999) '"Race", Racism and Education', in Hill, D. and Cole, M. (eds.) *Equality and Schooling: Conceptual and Empirical Issues.* Unpublished.

Index